Stop Barking and Start Leading

FIVE LEADERSHIP LESSONS WE CAN LEARN FROM MY DOG BENTLEY!

Robb Hiller

ISBN 13: 978-1-59298-950-8

Library of Congress Catalog Number: 2013921198

Printed in the United States of America

First Printing: 2014

17 16 15 14   5 4 3 2 1

Cover design by Vanessa Maynard
Interior design by Laura Drew
Cover photograph © Stu Bailey

Beaver's Pond Press
7108 Ohms Lane
Edina, MN 55439-2129
952-829-8818

To order, visit www.BeaversPondBooks.com
or call 1-800-901-3480. Reseller discounts available.

DEDICATION

I dedicate this book to my family and wonderful British lab, Bentley, who is an inspiration of "being who he is!" I am blessed to have a supportive wife, Pam, who loves me unconditionally, and three kids, Rick, Kate, and Ryan, who have totally enriched my life and helped make me a better husband, parent, and person.

ACKNOWLEDGMENTS

To My Editor—Steve LeBeau: I can't tell you how much I appreciate your work, which transformed my rough draft into a polished manuscript. You totally understood my ideas and made the whole process easy. I heartily recommend Steve to anyone thinking about writing a book. Thank you, Steve!

To the leaders who generously contributed their stories that contain great advice, thank you! Paul Harmel, CEO of Lifetouch; Rhoda Olsen, CEO of Great Clips; Mike Max, WCCO sports announcer; Jay Coughlin, CEO of XRS; Dennis Doyle, chairman of Welsh Companies; and Chris Wright, president of the Minnesota Timberwolves and Lynx, Greg Flack, former CEO of Schwans Food Company; and Doug Kohrs, former CEO of Tornier Medical and American Medical Systems.

I also want to thank the team at Beaver's Pond Press for their advice, their support, and pulling this project together. You guys are amazing and I am thankful for your support!

To My Mastermind Group: I have belonged to a mastermind group for years and can't think of a better group to thank for their inspiration, guidance, and help in so many ways. One day, my good friends Moss Jackson and Elizabeth Jeffries strongly encouraged me to get writing and put my passion onto paper. I didn't have a clue at that point what the book would be about. But after dinner one evening, I was off and running with ideas and a new passion.

RESOURCES TO HELP YOU:

SPREAD THE MESSAGE OF THIS MOVEMENT TO "KNOW WHO YOU ARE!"

I encourage you to go to my website, robbhiller.com, and download templates that will help you apply these five lessons and continue down the path to becoming a better person and leader. There are also other tools that you may find helpful at this website.

If you are interested in having me speak to your group, please contact me at 952-943-0747. (Please remember this is Central Time, Minneapolis, MN, and Bentley takes calls beginning at 8:00 AM!)

If you would like to set up a time to talk about how to engage and drive this positive message throughout your company with the many workshops available, I would love to talk with you. The company website is www.performancesolutionsmn.com.

MOST IMPORTANT, READ, ENJOY, AND APPLY THESE PROVEN TRUTHS IN THE BOOK!

CONTENTS

INTRODUCTION

After nearly eight years as the CEO of a high-tech company and eighteen years as an executive consultant, I can honestly say that the biggest problem faced by all businesses is *people*. The day after my company was sold, I felt a huge load had been lifted off my shoulders, because I was weighed down with people problems. Sure, I've struggled with strategy and marketing and sales, but the most widespread challenge has been people. Virtually every business leader I've met agrees with me.

But I've noticed something else. I've looked at successful businesses and wondered how they became so successful. It's the same answer: people! How can a company's biggest problems also be its biggest assets?

It took me years to figure it out, but once I did, the solution seemed rather simple and obvious. ***The difference between problem people and successful people is that successful people have tapped into their God-given talents and have been placed in positions where their talents can flourish.*** Unfortunately, it seems that about 70 percent of people do not know their own talents, or for some reason are unable to unleash them. What a waste!

Think what a difference it would make in total productivity if those 70 percent could be plugged into their natural talents. What if managers were able to select the right people and put them into appropriate positions to maximize their potential? You'd have a team full of self-motivated leaders! I have no doubt that it would jump-start the economy.

What we have now is the opposite. Not knowing one's own talent or that of others results in a huge business and personal cost for everyone. The general symptom is that of being *stuck*. The sales department gets stuck and growth suffers. People feel stuck and their morale seems to dry up and blow away. You have burnout, lack of personal accountability, lower sales, and lower profits. Everyone is dissatisfied.

Managers try to compensate by adding more heads to solve the issue, or they think they need to work harder and try to handle more tasks. Is that what's happening to you?

Are you so busy in back-to-back meetings that you have forgotten your many natural born talents and are ignoring them? **People today are so busy with overloaded schedules that the inevitable hamster treadmill just keeps going round and round.**

My solution? Don't be like that hamster. Try to be like my dog Bentley.

You've no doubt heard about Robert Fulghum's book, *All I Really Need to Know I Learned in Kindergarten.* For me it's more like, *All I need to know about leadership I learned from my dog Bentley.* Don't laugh, it's true!

My British lab is a role model because he is perfectly in tune with his natural talents, and he is happy to be himself. He's not full of existential angst or worry about whether he is doing the right thing. He is not misplaced and he doesn't try to be something he is not. He simply runs on instinct, and has a good time doing it. He is friendly and warm to everyone he meets, and every situation is brighter and happier when he is there. He is a natural leader!

Remember the passion and energy you had as a kid or early on in your career? Are you tired of feeling stuck? Are you longing to rekindle that fresh excitement? Maybe it's time to take another look at where your talents are today. If you are someone who wants to grow, believes you have much more to offer to the world, and wants to make a significant difference in what you are doing every day, you are a LEADER! Leadership is not a title, but an attitude with a commitment to be personally accountable.

The greatness of YOU lies in discovering and using the talents that nature has given to YOU. When we know and learn how to activate this incredible set of riches— our talents—we will naturally be led down our path of true meaning and realize better and more dynamic results.

When you are in your "talent zone," you can do almost anything. Watch the clouds lift and sun shine in when people are doing what my wonderful lab, Bentley, does every day—be who he is!

That is why I wanted to write this book, *Stop Barking and Start Leading.*

In this book you will see the simplicity and beauty of what a wonderful lab named Bentley can teach us about leading. These important lessons will uncomplicate both your business and personal lives, so that you can achieve greater success. We need to know who we are, be who we are, shake off our worries, and learn the joy of being a guide dog.

The purpose of this book is to help you rediscover your talents and help those on your team to do the same by following a five-step process, which I have presented in the first five chapters:

CHAPTER 1: HELLO, BENTLEY! KNOW WHO YOU ARE.

The first step toward becoming a true leader is to discover your hidden talents and find the real you. It is time to stop being so busy, so you can take some time to reflect on your true gifts. Maybe you knew your talents but forgot about them, or perhaps you need to do a self-inventory.

CHAPTER 2: THE GENTLE ART OF BEING BENTLEY. BE WHO YOU ARE.

Talent is like raw material; you need to make something out of it through practice. That's how skills are developed. The supreme karate expert Bruce Lee once said, *"I fear not the man who has practiced 10,000 kicks once, but I fear the man who has practiced one kick 10,000 times."* Activate your talents, and encourage others to activate theirs.

CHAPTER 3: UNLEASHING YOUR TALENTS! PRACTICE LEARNING NEW SKILLS.

Life is full of change and we are always learning. In order to keep going forward, you must develop creative leadership by learning new skills. Stay open to the wisdom of others and be coachable. True leadership is both flexible and accountable.

CHAPTER 4: DON'T LET IT BOTHER YOU; SHAKE IT OFF! PICK UP YOUR POOP!

Sometimes on the road to success, stuff happens. Keep your eyes on the prize and don't get distracted by trivial worries or errant emotions. To gain control of yourself, you need to acquire emotional intelligence and learn the art of forgiveness.

CHAPTER 5: BE A GUIDE DOG! THE JOY OF BRINGING OTHERS ALONG

Just as others have coached you, you need to learn to coach others. Good managers don't boss people around; they *engage* them. Guide them by inspiring them to manifest their talents.

If you struggle to be effective in your role today as I did for years as a CEO, this book is for you. You can change if you open up and discover the greatness within you and others on your team by following five lessons that my dog Bentley has taught me over the years.

ABOUT ROBB HILLER

After years of working for Xerox and a few other larger firms, I was one of the investors who took over a failing high-tech company, turned it around and sold it eight years later. After a six-month hiatus doing all the fun things I could think of, I decided to start the consulting company, Performance Solutions MN Inc., eighteen years ago. It is my belief that success is all about having the right people in the right jobs and growing their talent. Yes, strategy is important and part of my practice as a trusted advisor to executives and sales leaders, but the right talent and teamwork trump all.

Over these past years, I have helped many companies and people get "unstuck." It is my passion and I love it.

My vision for what I do: I help people and organizations discover how they can identify and ignite the use of their inborn talents to help them become what they are meant to be, and experience greater success.

CHAPTER 1

HELLO, BENTLEY! KNOW WHO YOU ARE.

Hello, Bentley!

When I say, "Hello, Bentley," my seven-year-old labrador knows I'm talking to him. He turns his head toward me, smiles as much as a dog can smile, and simultaneously his eyes flash open and say, "I'm glad to see you!" Bentley is our one family member who will never have an identity crisis. He knows he is the kind of dog who really likes people, and is always anxious to meet new people so he can share the love. He will run to you looking up, with his tail wagging, ready to cherish your attention. Bentley instinctively knows how to connect.

I was at the car dealership the other day to have my car washed, and Bentley joined me in the lounge while I waited. With his usual smile he sauntered in–without a leash–and came right to my side. A young woman who worked there saw Bentley and flashed a smile of her own. She shouted from across the room, "Can I come pet your beautiful dog? What's his name?"

"Sure," I replied. "You can pet Bentley." She rushed over and started to pet him. It was just for a minute or two, but all the while she just couldn't stop smiling and talking. Once again, Bentley was working his magic.

An older lady waiting for her car chimed in, "What a beauty!"

I quickly joked, "You mean me?"

She saw I was kidding and just laughed.

Everyone there was happier than they had been, thanks to Bentley. How does he do it? It's simple. He was born that way. You could say it's in his DNA or his instinct, but I like to view it as his God-given gift or talent. Bentley was born to be a people pleaser, and that's exactly what he loves to do. He doesn't try to be a guard dog and he doesn't pretend to be one. He is a loving lab whose goal is to make people happy by being who he is.

Seven years ago when my wife Pam, son Ryan, and I first went to pick out a new British lab, our hearts were open. Our old dog, Chamois, had recently died and we wanted another lab. The breeder pointed out two puppies for us to look at. She walked us over to an open meadow to let these two cuties show themselves off. The black puppy ran off instantly and let us know she was truly an adventurer. Ryan had limited success coaxing her over to play and cuddle. We could hardly touch her, but the yellow lab came over to us to be pet. Then he started playfully flopping over on the grass next to Ryan and rolled over and over. How fun! And what an entertainer! I had brought an old sock along, and as in a game I had often played with Chamois, threw it. The yellow lab immediately fetched it. He ran back and dropped it at my feet. He was a true-born retriever all right, an especially happy one. Pam, Ryan, and I just beamed with joy. It was a very easy decision, and that's how we met Bentley. Even as a little puppy, he aimed to please. He was born with it. He's added immeasurable joy to our household, and he brings joy with him everywhere he goes.

Why can't we all be like Bentley? Why can't we all be happy just by expressing our natural born talents? Why can't we all make everyone happy just by entering the room? **The sad truth is that most people have lost touch with who they are or have never discovered their valuable gifts in the first place.** Such people seldom experience the happiness of fulfilling their potential in a challenging environment; instead they feel the frustration of trying to be somebody they are not. They even begin to doubt whether they can ever be truly successful at all. Others may have a sense of their talents, but these remain forever hidden in the wrong job or the wrong position. It would be like locking Bentley in a kennel; he would no longer have the opportunity to share his gift of happiness. If we want to be like Bentley, we need to start exploring our inner selves to discover our true gifts. That's step number one. Know who you are.

Don't Copy This Xerox Experience

Early in my career I was hired to do sales for Xerox Corp. They recruited seven of us at the same time and spared no expense in flying us first class down to Leesburg, Virginia, for six weeks of training. They called our boot camp the Xeroid School. We were all very excited because it had a reputation for being the best in the world at training salespeople and leaders. We learned all about Xerography, products, speeds, paper types, applications, and–of course–we all enrolled in Sales 101.

After a few weeks of learning everything about the products and applications in our branch location, we were given a big test. Our manager/professor assigned each of us a small geographic territory, and then told us to visit every business in person and "sell them a Xerox copier." Those were his exact words. "Sell them a Xerox copier."

That particular advice didn't strike me quite right. That's not the way our Schwan's man did it when I was a kid. When I grew up in a small town in southwestern Minnesota, the Schwan's man with his truck of frozen food would drive right up to our house and greet my mom. He always smiled and asked her what the kids were eating these days. (He was referring to me and my two brothers—poor Mom!) That way he found out where there might be a fit for his products. My mom always called him "our Schwan's man." Needless to say, we ate a lot of Schwan's products and a ton of ice cream. I could see that he first of all established a friendly relationship, and then went on to serve our needs instead of pushing a product that his manager told him to sell. We didn't see him as a salesman but as part of our extended family. He was "*our* Schwan's man."

I recalled these memories as I knocked on doors all day.

At the end of the first day making cold calls on unsuspecting businesses, we all met back at the Xeroid School and were debriefed. I had made twenty sales calls and found a business whose office manager was sick and tired of their office's old, smelly electrostatic paper; she ordered a small Xerox 660. No other students had any prospects or orders from going out and trying to "sell a Xerox copier."

My colleagues—and even our manager—should have seen how our Schwan's man had handled the process of finding out what we needed and wanted. I was struck that one of the new sales recruits, Bernie, had made only five calls and none were successful. He gave many reasons for this lack of activity but the bottom line was that he really was not a salesperson. We confirmed that later when we all took an hour-long aptitude test. Bernie and two others didn't score the minimum seventy-two points, so they were driven to the airport and put on the next flight back to Minneapolis. The four of us who passed were put on the fast track, but it sure didn't seem like a very good percentage of success to me.

How painfully obvious for both the company and the people involved—it is clear to me now that these three did not know themselves and neither did the company. If only they had followed Bentley's nose! After a few sniffs, he would have learned that those three didn't have the right stuff to become salespeople. *Also, Bentley would have shown by example what our Schwan's man knew: The secret to sales and business in general is to build genuine human relationships. It's not that hard—if you simply follow your instincts and be yourself.*

But what if Bentley had been placed in the wrong job? What if he had been bought by a junkyard dealer and been put to work scaring away thieves and other dogs? I doubt that Bentley would be very successful. He'd rather play with the other dogs and let the thieves pet him. The junkyard dealer would say that Bentley was a terrible dog. I would have to disagree. Bentley is an excellent dog. He's just a lousy watchdog. And he knows it.

Soul Sapping

My Xerox incident left me with two indelible lessons. First, Bernie did not know himself. Whatever made him think he could possibly be a salesman? He was obviously not cut out for it. Secondly, why didn't our managers catch him earlier in the process? This easily could have been done by using more effective interview questions and a better assessment test. The pain of regret would never have taken root. Not to mention the expense of the first-class tickets and three weeks in Virginia and six weeks back in the branch training.

Bernie was not a fluke, either. My conversations with leaders agree with the results of the Right Management 2012 survey: Nearly 80 percent of people are dissatisfied with their jobs. Wow! It is obvious to me that many are unhappy because they are in the wrong jobs. No wonder we can feel personally stuck or see people on our teams who are not really excited about their jobs. That is sad and soul sapping! It means their true talents are locked away in a kennel with no place to shine.

What Is Talent?

A talent is an inborn capacity that makes people naturally highly successful in certain skilled activities. Some people are natural athletes, others are virtuosos at the piano, and yet others are born to sell. Tapping into your talent and expressing it through your actions is the recipe for a fruitful career and self-fulfillment. The key here is taking action. It reminds me of when the sales rep asks, "When will I get my raise?" And the boss quickly replies, "Your raise is effective when you are!"

If you don't identify your talents and exercise them, you won't develop your skills. The best athlete in the world had to practice many hours to become good. Talent is not something you sit on; it atrophies if you don't exercise it.

Philosophers and religious leaders in the ancient world knew the importance of finding talents and developing potential. When Greeks sought wisdom, they went to the Oracle at Delphi, where the inscription read, "Know Thyself." Socrates upped the ante and said, "The unexamined life is not worth living." Aristotle, in his teaching on ethics, advised that the way to achieve happiness is by developing inborn talent.

The importance of nurturing personal talent was even

the topic for one of the famous parables of Jesus of Nazareth. In the book of Matthew, He tells the story of a man going on a journey who entrusts his wealth to three of his servants. The distribution depends on their abilities, so one servant gets five talents of gold, another gets two, and the person with the least ability gets only one talent of gold. When their master returns, the servants report what has transpired in his absence. The first two servants had used the gold and invested in various enterprises with good result. They each doubled their wealth, with one servant returning ten talents of gold and the other returning four. The master praised these industrious servants and welcomed them to share his happiness.

The third servant had feared for the safety of the gold, so he buried his lone talent, and returned it to his master intact yet unused. The master scolded this servant for not realizing the value he possessed, and thereupon threw him out into the street where he cried forlorn in the darkness.

The beauty of a parable is that it can be understood at different levels. At the literal level it is a story that praises investment; you have to use money to make money. But the parable of the talents can also be understood at a metaphorical level. In those days, a talent was a unit of measurement for precious metals. The word "talent" initially meant "weight," from the proto-Indo-European root "tol," which is where we get our word "toll," as in a tollbooth. So the number of talents of gold literally refers to how much it weighs. But on a metaphorical level, the value of the gold is the inner potential we have as human beings. That's the sense that Jesus used for a second level of meaning in His parable. In other words, our talents are precious gifts, innate abilities that are meant to be used. If we don't use them, we are lost in the darkness with no direction.

Plato used the same metaphor when he attempted to construct an ideal society. The key, he said, was to give every person a different role based on their natural talents. He said there are gold people, silver people, and bronze people. A harmonious society emerges when they all do work that fits their natural talents. I think the same holds true in any organization. Your chances of success increase substantially if you have the right talents in the proper positions.

Wherefore Art Thou, O Talent?

"To thine own self be true, and it must follow, as the night the day, thou canst not then be false to any man."
—William Shakespere

If the greatest minds of western civilization agreed on the importance of self-discovery and self-actualization, why aren't we better at finding and realizing our talents? Once again, why can't we be more like Bentley? His love of retrieving objects was a genetic inheritance. I never had to teach him to chase after a bone, a ball, a shoe, a newspaper, or a Frisbee. He was simply designed to love doing these things with ease. Like the Robert Redford baseball movie, *The Natural,* the name says it all! Can't we learn to return to our natural instincts?

After all, it is a travesty seeing a person who thinks she should do something that she is not really gifted to do, while ignoring her actual talents. How many times have you known someone who had a lot of innate talent but it never seemed to blossom? While simple ignorance of their innate gifts can block some people from full expression, others are in denial for various reasons. These are the really tough cases—people who have an inkling of their gifts, but don't follow through.

Often they have a fear of failure or some lack of personal accountability. Perhaps a negative experience from the past is holding them back. Various factors conspire to cause people to lock themselves in kennels, where they promptly feel trapped because they have forgotten that they have the keys to get themselves out. Our job in this book is to remind you that you possess the key, and then to show you how to unlock your cage. Regardless of where you are in your career, it is never too late to learn to appreciate your God-given gifts.

The Leadership Connection: Leadership Is Not a Title, It's an Attitude!

There are two types of people in the world: those who lead, and those who are led. Which are you? Don't think you have to be an executive or a manager at a company to be a leader. I believe all self-directed people deserve to be called leaders if they actively express their talent, want to improve, and make a difference where they are today. For example, I know of some executive assistants who are so skilled at their positions that the CEO would be lost without them. Conversely, the CEO can be gone for two weeks and everything runs smoothly, because the executive assistant is on top of things. Ideally, every employee at a company can become a leader and learn to be a positive influence in every situation they enter. Such a business is bound to be successful. If, on the other hand, you are holding back on your talents or are locked into an inappropriate position, you can feel inside that something is wrong. This friction between the real you and the false you sometimes results in a growl or a bark, or maybe just a frequent whimper. You are on someone else's leash, and it irritates you.

The most profound result of using your natural talents is that you become a leader. Your self-confidence motivates your actions without following a script written by someone else for a part you were never intended to play. You are an actor, playwright, and director, free to create your own destiny. Otherwise you are stuck, and can only follow. Or as Bentley would say, "Stop barking and start leading."

The Rise and Fall of Jane

What about business executives who are seasoned and have been around the block? Do years of experience make that big of a difference in knowing oneself? In my eighteen years of working with executives and managers, I would say mostly NO. *Business people who have some level of success often get so busy that they stop growing and learning.* They are swallowed up in the daily grind of meetings, travel, and the pressure to get it done *now*! If they have a moment to stop and think, they ask themselves, "When do I get the time to reflect and learn how to be more effective?"

That's what happened to Jane, a charming and friendly director of marketing who was key to her company's growth for its first seven years. But then her department stalled, she quit getting results, and her people started missing deadlines. The grumbling grew and management reached out to get her back on course. However, nothing worked.

The CEO asked me to help, so I met with her. Here was a successful, goal-driven woman who had somehow lost her moorings. I asked her a simple question: "Would you like to discover your greatness?"

Jane immediately said, "Yes!"

"Tell me why," I asked.

She told me her story and all about her current job predicament. She believed deep down that she could do better, but she just felt stuck. It was obvious that her leadership skills had weakened because she was no longer being self-directed by using her innate talents.

I asked her point blank: "Do you want to discover your greatness so you can become the leader and influencer you are meant to be?"

Jane couldn't wait to get started on a process of self-discovery. She took a full set of assessments that revealed her leadership style, motivating values, talent, and emotional intelligence. As we went over the results, Jane was surprised to learn that she had been unaware of her many strengths, as well as her weaker areas. The more we talked the more she could see that she had lost control of her situation because she was not in touch with herself. But now she had taken the first step toward getting unstuck. She was getting to know the real Jane. The end result was that she flourished in her role for the next two years and really made a difference in the company.

Jane's case is far from unique. Nine times out of ten, when a company finds projects that are not getting done, the reason is that its team members are not getting along. They don't function as a team because some key people are not very good at what they do. Usually these people were promoted to their positions, but dropped into slots where they didn't fit. You can solve two problems at once by pulling them out of there and putting them in new slots where they can excel, slots that better fit their talents.

Let's Get Started

The good news is that even though many people have lost touch with their true talents, psychologists and social scientists have conducted a lot of research into human personality and our inborn skills. They have created various maps and charts to explore the human psyche in the form of tests and assessments to guide self-discovery. It is a lot easier to embark on this life-changing journey if you have a map!

So, let's begin your discovery and follow Bentley's idea of leading by knowing better who you are. I will ask you the same question I asked Jane, "Do you want to discover your greatness so you can become the leader and influencer you are meant to be? If so, let's begin."

Here is a mini-starter assessment that you can conduct by yourself, which is far simpler than the full battery of assessments that are available for more intensive use. If you want to complete the full twenty-four-page version, visit the website noted at the back of book to see how you can do so.

Step I: These are roughly half the choices of a full assessment, but they can give you guidance. For each row, circle one of the four words which best describes you. Count the number of circles in each column and total at the bottom. Check the style at the bottom that has the highest total. Now look at the strengths of this style! (See chart on opposite page)

Step II: Your Behavioral Style Score: The highest number is your primary behavior inclination and the second highest is your secondary behavioral inclination. These descriptors give you guidance as to your primary talents of your style.

Step III: Based on your primary style, how can you use your talents more each and every day? Write down some key ideas now!

1.

2.

3.

Behavioral Style Exercise

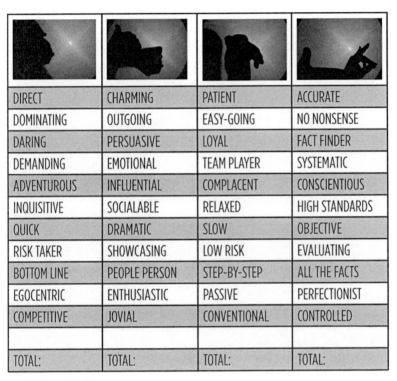

DIRECT	CHARMING	PATIENT	ACCURATE
DOMINATING	OUTGOING	EASY-GOING	NO NONSENSE
DARING	PERSUASIVE	LOYAL	FACT FINDER
DEMANDING	EMOTIONAL	TEAM PLAYER	SYSTEMATIC
ADVENTUROUS	INFLUENTIAL	COMPLACENT	CONSCIENTIOUS
INQUISITIVE	SOCIALABLE	RELAXED	HIGH STANDARDS
QUICK	DRAMATIC	SLOW	OBJECTIVE
RISK TAKER	SHOWCASING	LOW RISK	EVALUATING
BOTTOM LINE	PEOPLE PERSON	STEP-BY-STEP	ALL THE FACTS
EGOCENTRIC	ENTHUSIASTIC	PASSIVE	PERFECTIONIST
COMPETITIVE	JOVIAL	CONVENTIONAL	CONTROLLED
TOTAL:	TOTAL:	TOTAL:	TOTAL:

copyright @TTI Success Insights Inc.

☐ **GORILLA**   ☐ **HOUND**   ☐ **CAMEL**   ☐ **DEER**

Your Mini-360

Scottish poet Robert Burns yearned for the ability to see himself as others saw him. It is a bit unsettling to think that other people may know us better than we know ourselves, but at the same time, that's a remarkable resource for us on our journey. As you embark on your transformation into a leader, get a little help from your friends, people who can be objective and sincere in their appraisals of you. A 360 analysis, as its name suggests, sets out to look at a situation from every angle. For your mini-360, you begin with at least two important perspectives: your subjective viewpoint, and someone else's objective viewpoint. If you get more than one person to give their assessment of you, so much the better!

Change is scary for many people, and it is often more comfortable to stay cozy and locked up in your kennel than to go out and face a strange new world. Once you overcome that fear, it is exciting to think you can make a change for the better. The same internal energy that drives your fear gets rechanneled to drive your passion for improvement. It's all a matter of attitude, and it becomes easy to make the switch.

Many executives get the idea right away—once I have spoken with them about the need to find the hidden talents of their employees. Its truth is obvious, but they needed someone to point it out. That's all it takes for most of us. Once you begin to know the real you, you get excited and refreshed. There is a lot to like about the real you, and it will feel good to get started.

Easy Suggestions to Implement Now!

Email the following questions to co-workers with whom you have a good relationship, and at least one good friend. Preface the email with this short introduction as to why you are asking for their feedback. (This template can be downloaded from the www.robbhiller.com website.)

Dear _____, I am reading a book called *Stop Barking and Start Leading: 5 Leadership Lessons We Can Learn From My Dog Bentley* by Robb Hiller, and the first lesson is gaining a perspective of how people view my talents. Would you take a moment and respond back today? Thanks so much, as this will be of real value to me.

1- What do you feel are my strongest talents?
2- The book defines leadership in this way: "Leadership is not a title, it's an attitude!" Do you see my actions as wanting to get better with a strong desire to make a difference in what I am doing?
3- Do you feel I am personally accountable? Coachable? Any examples?
4- Do you have any suggestions that would encourage me in my development?

Thanks so much for sharing. Oh yes, Bentley, thanks you as well!

The Next Step: Actualization

Knowing who you really are and becoming aware of your true talents is the first step on our path. But as we mentioned above, following up with action is essential. Raw talent doesn't mean a thing if you don't take that swing. The next step is to manifest your talent by engaging in activities where they can flourish. That is the topic of Chapter 2.

Scientists define learning for all creatures as the interaction between instinct and environment. It's not nature *versus* nurture; it's nature *and* nurture. This tells us two things right away. First, you have to act. Secondly, you have to act in a nourishing environment that allows your talents to grow to their full potential. Just as in real estate, it comes down to three things: location, location, location.

If two salespeople are thrown into the same territory, the one who does not have the right profile for that product will falter, even if she tries hard and does all the right things, and she's a nice person. But if you throw the right person into that sales territory, usually within three months she will have raised sales by 20 percent. It's a matter of talent properly matched to an environment, an interactive situation that becomes very practical indeed. It's about unleashing your innate ability to go forth and influence the outcomes of your interactions. It feels so wonderful yet it is also totally natural. Just ask Bentley, who will tell you that the secret is simply being who you are. When you unleash your inborn gifts, people will light up and elevate everyone.

Paw Prints to Remember

- Knowing more of who you are is the key to finding your passion and purpose in life; self-knowledge can help you to be more genuine and successful at whatever you are doing.

- When you actualize your natural talents, customers are more likely to love you and want more of you! Are you affectionately referred to by your customer as "theirs?" Do all the members of your team know their talents and feel the same way?

- Don't be a "Soul Sapper!" Knowing your talents allows you to develop a vision and enables you to put yourself in the right role or job. Get yourself and others on the team in the appropriate positions.

- Don't be like the servant in the parable who buried his talent and became lost in the wilderness! Use your talents the way they were meant to be used.

CHAPTER 2

THE GENTLE ART OF BEING BENTLEY!
BE WHO YOU ARE.

That's a Good Boy, Bentley!

It's a delight to watch Bentley's natural skills at work as he spreads joy to our family and the people he happens to meet. The gentle art of being Bentley, though, flourishes because his actions are rewarded and encouraged. For Bentley to manifest his natural love, he carries out actions: he acts and reacts. That is an important lesson for us on our path to leadership. For our talents to grow, we need to be encouraged.

On a recent summer afternoon our family dined on the outdoor deck of a restaurant, and of course Bentley joined us, sitting calmly by our side. He's a part of the family, after all! Some young children at a nearby table were intrigued by Bentley and started to approach him. A two-year-old boy walked over and looked at Bentley, wondering if he could pet him. My wife Pam turned to the child and said, "You can pet Bentley, go ahead."

He slowly put his hand out to do so and Bentley gently lifted his head up to be petted. The little boy shrieked briefly with surprise, but then his five-year-old sister rushed over and fearlessly gave Bentley a big hug. Bentley stood up wagging his tail like a fly swatter on overdrive, and the love fest began! A one-year-old just learning to walk joined the others and Bentley immediately sensed that the toddler was hesitant, so he lowered himself down to his level. How considerate. All of a sudden, the five-year-old girl asked us, "Could we take Bentley for a walk around the deck?" We said, "Sure." Bentley joined them as they gleefully paraded around this huge deck. All the kids were giggling and having a ball following Bentley, our natural leader.

After the kids returned Bentley to us and went back to their table, their parents walked over and thanked us profusely. They said, "Your dog really made our day! Our kids couldn't be happier!"

I was proud of Bentley for another remarkable display of his natural talent, but then I wondered, "Bentley is such a giving creature. What does he get out of it? What keeps him going?" I realized that Bentley gets plenty of encouragement from the humans he interacts with. Each time he is petted, or hugged, or praised, it is a small reward that reinforces his behavior. He continues to act the way he does because it works. He gets plenty of loving attention, plus a nice home and regular meals. No wonder he keeps it up!

The same principle holds for other members of Bentley's species that go to obedience school to learn how to behave properly or to learn tricks. Each time they display a behavior correctly, they get a reward such as a doggie treat, a pat on the head, or a kind word of praise. Giving positive attention and encouragement really works to develop one's inborn talents.

Encouraging My Gift of Song—A Lesson on Values For Leaders

When I was eight years old my parents found a way to encourage one of my natural talents. I was never sure whether this was a random whim or they did it on purpose, but it made a big difference in my life. We were visiting my grandparents in Detroit Lakes, Minnesota, for the weekend. All the relatives were sitting around the living room just talking casually, when my mother suddenly came up with an idea. She said, "Robby, would you like to earn some money so you can go down to the corner store and get some candy?"

Well, that is like asking Bentley if he wants to be pet. Of course I did!

My mom had always enjoyed hearing me sing in church, so she said, "Why don't you grab grandma's cup and sing one of the songs from Sunday school? Then let's see if any of your relatives want to make a donation."

I thought for a moment and immediately the song "Jesus Loves Me" came to my mind. I sang the first verse in my finest soprano voice, aiming to please. When I finished, everyone clapped and put some money in the cup as I passed it around. Talk about instant gratification!

Now, I did not know whether I actually had a musical gift at this point, but the strong response was more than just the relatives being nice. I apparently did have some talent and this was the first time it was *activated* because people paid positive attention to me. I collected all the coins, put them into my pocket, and took off for the candy store a few blocks away. Wow, this was pure bliss for me! M&M's, Bit-O-Honey bites, and Snickers never tasted so good! I learned that people really did like hearing me sing and they actually rewarded me with praise and enough money to buy something I liked. These simple rewards—applause, praise, money, and candy—brought me confidence in my gift. It encouraged me to develop my singing for years to come.

Developing Your Gift

I was fortunate that my parents were always there to encourage me to explore my gifts, but not everyone is so lucky. A recent article in the *Minneapolis Star Tribune* tells the story of a young man who has become a star football player for the University of Minnesota Gophers. As a young boy he had a sense of his athletic talents, but received neither the encouragement nor the stability in his life to develop his skills. Social services removed the boy from his mother, a drug addict who was arrested for possession. The system sent him through a series of unwelcoming foster homes—eleven in all—and the only thing he developed was a sense of frustration and a bitter attitude. But he never abandoned his sense that he had a purpose in life, so in a video he made for prospective adoptive parents, he said, "I want a family that will let me play football."

At last his wish was granted. A stable upper-middle class couple that encouraged him to play football adopted him. His talents flourished in high school, but it wasn't easy. He had an identity crisis at times because he was African American and his adoptive parents were white, something his black friends didn't always understand. Yet when he graduated from high school and a number of colleges wanted to recruit him, he chose to stay close to home and his support network; he joined the Gophers.

His hard work has made him a team leader. His talent developed because it was encouraged and allowed to grow. He was rewarded by praise, recognition, and a college scholarship. Plus, as a star defensive tackle, he saw immediate results from his actions in the form of sacked quarterbacks and tackled ball carriers. His talents may lead to him being selected as a first round draft pick upon graduation. If all goes well, his next reward will be a lucrative NFL contract. But even if this doesn't materialize, this athlete has repeatedly said that he is blessed because he has found his talents, has worked hard at his craft, is committed to making a difference, and has been encouraged from his coaches and adopted parents. He is a leader.

Practice Makes Perfect

After my debut as an eight-year-old soloist, I spent many years developing my gift for singing. In high school I sang and played guitar in a special traveling group called "The Roaring 20s" and I also won a statewide music competition. Such rewards prompted me to continue to sing in college. That's one reason I selected St. Olaf College, a small liberal arts school in Northfield, Minnesota, with one of the foremost a cappella choral groups in the nation— the St. Olaf Choir. It was world famous both for the quality of the singing as well as for its vast and challenging repertoire. With the encouragement of my professors I finally earned a spot in this prestigious group. Membership in this elite choir was a reward in itself, but we were also rewarded by performing all across the country. We traveled and sang in places like the Dorothy Chandler Pavilion, which hosted the Academy Awards more than twenty times, and at the Moscone Center in San Francisco. For our efforts we received praise from audiences and critics alike.

Leadership Lesson—Making It Look Easy

This intense experience gave me two valuable lessons about developing talent. First, it takes a lot of work to make it look easy. Learning to use your voice—or any other instrument—goes through two stages. At first you pay heavy attention to each specific thing, such as the notes of a new song or the strings on guitar, or even the keys on a typewriter. Then you repeat the activity so many times that it becomes a habit and you don't think about the specifics anymore. After the notes become habitual and automatic, you can focus on the meaning of the music, you become an interpreter, and you are ready for the performance. Our job as entertainers was to make the music sound natural and smooth, belying the many hours we put into practice. The football team began in August and was done by late November. The basketball team also worked together for four months. But the St. Olaf Choir was a year-round activity. We practiced five days a week for the entire year.

The second lesson I learned was about the magic of harmonious group activity. Our individual talents melted into a spiritual oneness when we sang perfectly together. When everyone was in tune and we felt totally connected with each other, a special feeling emerged. It was an experience of synergy, where the totality was more than the sum of its parts. It was a wonderful sensation, and it also produced beautiful music that the audiences *loved*. They didn't simply *like* us; they *loved* us.

While our choir literally harmonized together, teams in sports and businesses also excel when they achieve a similar sense of spiritual oneness. Two football teams could be evenly matched in terms of individual talent, but if one team achieves that perfect sense of harmonious collaboration, they will run away with the game. It won't even be close. Spectators can feel that magic; they can almost see it. Everything seems to go right for the harmonious teams. You can also feel this special harmony in businesses where all the workers collaborate in a seamless synergy. Their individual talents merge to form something bigger than all of them. Clients and customers can feel that sensation, and they love it. It's the kind of magnetic pull that builds loyalty, and that needs to be encouraged in every team. If you visit a company, sit in on a team meeting, or walk through a factory, you can catch the spirit of what is going on. It's like running into Bentley on a summer afternoon: you can instantly feel the love.

The Magic of Leading With Love

This spiritual dimension of harmonious group activity is so strong that if anyone happens to be slightly out of tune, it's as nerve-wracking as fingernails on a chalkboard. Your skin crawls and it makes you shudder. Being close to the note doesn't count. In the choir we were taught to help each other through such dissonance. If the person next to us was even a little bit flat or sharp, we would nudge that person with an elbow or, during a concert, we discreetly squeezed their hand. As members of the team we were all responsible; we were all leaders. Any of us could break the harmony, or restore it.

And remember, a leader is someone who knows his or her talent, takes action, is committed to getting better, and wants to make a difference! Within a team, the ideal case is when everyone plays their role exceptionally to the best of their talent. Everyone is playing the same tune and hearing the same drummer. That's when the magical unity lifts everything to a higher harmonic level. That is the art of actualizing your talents.

Vocation or Avocation?

It is easy to believe that your unique set of talents is a perfect match for some vocation in life, a career in which you develop your innate gifts and at the same time earn a living. If your talent is fulfilling but does not serve as a source of income, it becomes a hobby or avocation for you. It may be intrinsically important as one of your gifts, but it doesn't offer that monetary reward that everyone needs in life. It is not always easy to make the distinction, in which case experience may be the best teacher.

That's what happened to me and my love of singing. After college I had followed the practical path in my career choice and had become the CEO of a small high-tech company. I had achieved real success, but I didn't feel fulfilled. There was a yearning inside of me to sing again, and perhaps to find out once and for all whether my talent was sufficiently strong to make a career of it.

Then I heard about a music talent contest called the National Christian Artists Competition. This was similar to the talent shows on TV today such as *The Voice*. I decided to enter the competition and flew out to Estes Park, Colorado, for the event. Little did I know that being 8,000 to 9,000 feet above sea level definitely affects a singer's breathing capacity. Let's just say the air is rather thin, and not as nutritious and filling as Minnesota air. I was gasping for breath the first day but managed to make it to the finals by the end of day three. I was probably the oldest contestant, but I didn't care. I was there because I felt that the joy of singing in this environment would make me better and I wanted to see where it would take me.

I finished fifth in my category and was thrilled to do so well. My performance had attracted a talent scout from Benson Records and we made a record in Nashville, Tennessee. Yes, in those days we actually made music on tapes and CDs! I flew into Nashville for my recording session with the Nashville Symphony as my back up. On the first day of the session I was so in awe of their talent that I forgot the words at first. As I relaxed and started to sing, their flawless talent lifted me to a new level. When I first heard the playback I got tears in my eyes. Here was a virtual nobody singing with this group of pros and the result was beautiful music. What a difference to work with that level of talent!

My recordings began to be played on radio stations across the country, and I was invited to sing on some TV shows. In fact, one of my songs briefly reached the Top 20 on the music charts. But I soon learned that a good singing voice and passion for the music is not enough to make a career of it. You also need good material. It's like a good actor who only appears in bad films. He needs a good script to make it big, and I needed good songs. Many novice singers bridge this gap by writing their own songs, a talent that I did not possess. I tried, but it was too painful to even think about. The alternative was to be famous so that good songwriters brought their songs to me. For me, it was a Catch-22. I needed good songs to become famous, but since I wasn't famous, I couldn't get good songs. I realized that singing was a gift to be shared, but it wasn't my calling. Singing was to be my avocation.

Professor Failure

This wasn't my first failure, nor thankfully was it my last. Failure has been a constant instructor to me and has given me feedback as to what I need to do. Failure has allowed me to avoid certain areas to some degree and to just walk away from others. That is another talent that I believe most people should foster—the ability to learn from your mistakes. Over the years, I have had many, many failures and that has been a good thing!

Earlier in life I fancied the idea of becoming a golf pro, until I ran into Professor Failure. I really enjoy going out to play golf on a beautiful course, with the smell of the freshly cut grass and the fellowship of being with other people for a brief four-hour escape. It is heavenly. The only problem is my talent. I am decent at golf, but to play at a professional level... Help! Get me out of here!

This fact became obvious when I was seventeen and playing on my high school golf team. In one tournament I had to win the eighth hole to continue to play. That hole had a river running through it and was a par 3 at around 160 yards. I stepped up to the tee and promptly choked, hitting the ball right into the river. That little splash was the sound of my golf career going underwater. At the same time this was a wake-up splash, a lesson to be heeded about my direction in life. Hint: this wasn't it!

That meant it was time to search for a new path, a new fence to climb, a new field to explore. For failure leads to a type of learning that only comes from experience, you can't learn it in a book. It leads to the deeper kind of understanding that Solomon called wisdom, the ability to make good decisions on the road of life. As we go on that journey, wisdom helps us to find our purpose in life. It's not easy, but wisdom makes it possible.

Somewhere out there in the future I knew there was a spark, a flash of light that could ignite my talents. A little water trap wasn't going to stop me from someday sending fireworks exploding in the sky. Someday I'd find my personal Fourth of July and light up my corner of the world with my God-given gifts—whatever they might be.

How to Genuinely Please Your Boss

You have to keep searching until you find your buried talents, and let them loose to grow and develop. Then you are on the right path as a contributing leader in every situation. Why then do some people insist on hiding their light under a barrel whenever they are around the boss? Your talents combined with those of your boss should be the recipe for natural synergy, but it only works if you are genuine. Whether out of fear or some misguided shyness, some employees can't be straightforward with their boss-es and don't say what is really on their minds. They only try to say what they think the boss wants to hear, and they keep their valid but candid opinions to themselves.

Over the past eighteen years, the top leaders of many companies have told me that they just love people who are genuine, results oriented and straightforward. A pres-ident of one company recently said the one thing that really bugged him about his sales leader was that, "He just gives me BS instead of being honest with me." The salesman is a great guy, but he is useless at truly serving his boss. The president said he lowers his expectations when he talks with this salesman, and has to try to distin-guish the truth from the other stuff.

Why don't we simply be who we are?

How Your Boss Can Genuinely Please You

Sometimes it's the other way around. You may be per-fectly prepared to be direct with your boss and share your talents with the company—only the boss is oblivious to your talents. How do you handle a difficult boss? First, call Bentley and he can take you for a long walk. This will give you time to calm down and let loose of your frustra-tion. After a short time, you will be smiling, laughing, and just enjoying the experience of being with someone who can bring the best out in you. Bentley will remind you to simply be yourself. So what is your next step?

One of the main reasons people leave companies is because they have a lousy boss. When that happens, you have to become the leader of the situation. Just as the singer who gets off key needs a little elbow in the ribs, sometimes your boss needs a little reminder to get in tune with you. My advice is to take the initiative and sit down with your boss to have him or her participate in this discovery process you are going through. Make an appointment for at least a forty-five-minute meeting so you won't be rushed or interrupted. You may want to share the feedback you have received from doing your own mini-360 from Chapter 1. Perhaps you can ask your boss to do the behavioral exercise and then compare your similarities and differences. This little effort will open up communication in a whole new way.

Second, share the simple exercise involving the six motivating values at the end of this chapter, since these are fundamental to your talents and what inspires your actions. Finally, list your strengths and give your boss ideas on how to best make use of your talents. It is up to you! This is being 100 percent personally accountable. You can't change your boss, but you can be proactive and engage him or her in a wonderful discussion that may open up other ideas and opportunities that you two had never thought about. And remember Bentley's advice—just be you!

Beware of Ghosts

Sometimes harmony in the workplace is corrupted by ghosts, hidden personality disorders, or dysfunctions caused by past incidents that live deep inside of you. I saw this once while consulting for a software company. It was obvious that the founder, a technical guru named Mike, related to people in a totally different way than Paul, the company president. For one thing, they had different personalities. Mike was an introvert who had a difficult time with communication, meeting deadlines, and getting along with people. Paul was a friendly extrovert. On the second day of our offsite strategy planning session, I noticed that Mike was becoming agitated. It got so bad that by midday he blew up at what one of the other leaders was saying and he walked out in a huff. I called an hour recess and went outside with Paul and Mike to try to understand what was going on with Mike.

Both Paul and I listened to what he had to say, and after a while he calmed down. We returned and finished the meeting. What became obvious is that Mike functioned better one-on-one than in a group, where he somehow felt threatened. Instead of just accepting or contemplating the consensus of ideas coming from the group, Mike reacted defensively. Whenever he sensed conflict he lost all reason and reverted to a primitive jungle persona. He became like a tyrannical gorilla, pounding on his chest to assert his dominance.

Afterwards I met Mike for a beer and some informal conversation. I wanted to find out why he felt so betrayed and why he hated being told what to do by the group. He finally shared the real reason. It turns out he had a painful and tormented childhood because his father harshly criticized everything he did. Why wasn't he doing better in school? Why wasn't he better in sports? Why wasn't he doing everything that his father thought he should do? I felt his anguish as he told his sad story. I finally asked him if he wanted to continue to be kenneled up with these feelings of fear and rejection.

He said "No," so we took some time to review his full leadership profiles. We focused on how he could activate his talents to strengthen his sense of self-control. Why should he still be haunted by his father when he could grow out of it by asserting his gift?

It was somewhat amazing to see that once he had identified the hidden enemies of fear, doubt and rejection, he was able to focus on being who he really was. He improved his behavior quite a bit, even though his demons still flared up occasionally. But when they did, he at least he could recognize what was going on and had a vocabulary and a thought process to deal with it. His efforts lowered the tension of the entire team and enabled real progress. Like Bentley, Mike actually became happier, and the dreaded gorilla did not come out that often. The key was focusing on what he did really well and getting this out in the open. The result was a much more fun and healthy environment!

Activating My Gifts and Talents Exercise

1- To activate your gifts, look back at the two exercises in Chapter 1 and write down your discoveries in a simple list.

   a. My talents are:

   b. The common theme seems to be:

   c. Areas I might have thought about but have not focused on as talents of mine:

   d. Other:

2- Answer the following basic questions regarding your motivating values and add this to your list. (See the motivating values exercise below.)

3- Share this information with at least two or three people you trust to gain feedback.

4- If you want a better relationship with your boss, share this information and the book with them!

5- Oh yes, and if you really have courage, share a few of these types of coaching questions that your boss might ask to help engage a better conversation! Or, if you are a boss, you may consider asking each person these questions to build a company where inspiring "love" can be the difference between success and failure.

   a. Where is your passion today?

b. What talents do you most enjoy using?

c. What types of roles or assignments are the most exciting for you today?

d. How would you best describe your behavioral style? (See Chapter 1 exercise.)

e. What motivates you?

f. What talent or skill might need to be developed, or which ones are not activated like they could be?

g. How can I be of help to you?

Motivating Values Exercise

There are six basic types of workplace motivators!

The following comes from research done by German philosopher and psychologist Eduard Spranger, which he described in his 1928 classic, "Types of Men." This research became famous and is used today in a very detailed twenty-five-page assessment tool I have used with clients. Here are some basics to guide you in this important discovery. As you think through these descriptions, circle your top two that best represent why you get up every day and do things that give you intrinsic satisfaction.

Theoretical: This is wanting answers, facts, data, truth, and sharing this knowledge for problem solving. People who have a passion for this enjoy reading, doing research, solving problems with facts, data, and logic.

Utilitarian: One who has this motivator just loves the return on investment, thinking in everything one does. A utilitarian just wants everything to be useful and productive and likes that there is a financial reward as part of their drive. Money can many times be viewed as keeping score, but practicality is just as important.

Aesthetic: This motivating value likes things being

harmonious; desiring things to feel good, look good, and be pleasing overall. This could be artistic, creative, or subjective in nature.

Social: People with a strong social motivator just love to help others to become more of who they are, and see potential. They love to solve people problems like poverty, homelessness, and other issues.

Individualistic: A person with this motivating value likes to be at the table when decisions are being made and want to be seen as a leader whose voice is heard. They are connectors of people and want to be recognized if they do a good job. They are intensely strong goal setters and want to drive change when needed.

Traditional: This motivating value is about wanting to follow instruction and procedures. It is a system for living. A person with this motivating value sees the world in black and white terms and not too many shades of gray. They want things done correctly, with quality and they believe in a higher power.

My top two motivating values are:

1- _____

2- _____

1. Now ask yourself these simple questions and then create a conversation with your peers, team members, and boss: How does this impact my actions and decisions on a daily basis?

2. Does my role or job today allow these motivating values to be used and rewarded on a daily basis? If not,

where could they be?

3. Are there additional projects that I could make others and my boss aware of that would tap into these motivating values? Please share!

Paw Prints To Remember

🐾 People are key to helping us discover our God-given talents. So begin to ask for feedback.

🐾 When you stop barking and discover more of who you are, you will be in tune!

🐾 Being in tune activates the collective gifts of everyone with *practice*.

🐾 Welcome failure as a teacher. It can be *the guide you need.*

🐾 You will please your boss, peers, and yourself when you *be who you are.*

🐾 Focusing on your talents can overcome the enemies of fear, doubt, and rejection.

CHAPTER 3

UNLEASHING YOUR TALENTS! PRACTICE LEARNING NEW SKILLS.

What's New, Bentley?

Bentley aims to please; that's what he lives for. But people sometimes get bored with the same old thing, so Bentley is constantly coming up with new ways to please people. He is always learning new tricks because he instinctively knows that a true leader is constantly going forward.

One day I was playing fetch with Bentley, and as he brought back the rubber ball, he looked in my eyes. He wanted to see if I was pleased. Maybe my smile wasn't big enough for him, but for some reason he figured he needed to do something novel. He suddenly started spinning around in circles, as if he were doing doggie ballet. I laughed out loud when I saw him dancing around and around, so he knew I was pleased. I liked it so much I started encouraging him to keep doing it by calling out, "Go, Bentley, go!" It worked; the more I kept saying it, the more Bentley danced.

Now, Bentley dances whenever I say "Go, Bentley, go." When the kids come over I tell Bentley to "Go, Bentley, go," and as he starts spinning, the children burst out laughing and can't stop giggling. They are totally mesmerized by this natural leader who never stops manifesting his limitless talent by learning new skills.

As I mentioned in Chapter 2, there is an important lesson for us on our paths to leadership. For our talents to grow, we need to be encouraged to unleash our gifts. In this chapter, we look at ways to unleash new skills so we never stop going forward.

Such progress comes from retrieving, practicing, and developing our talents. This means we need to be coachable and accountable. This is where I believe many leaders and executives fall down, because they have forgotten what got them to their current successful positions. For example, when was the last time you sat down and wrote out a list of your key talents and put them out in front of you? We tend to take our talents for granted and forget about them, when we should be taking inventory of them every day. For all too many executives, it has been a long time since they have thought about their natural strengths.

It's an especially good thing to remember your talents when you are stuck and really need to start making progress. Don't let the wellspring of your success get buried in the past. Retrieve it and start doing something new with it to get you moving again.

Be Coachable and Trainable If You Want to Go Somewhere

One of Bentley's wonderful traits is his eagerness to improve with coaching from us. I got tired of always walking out to the driveway every morning to get the newspaper, so I decided to train Bentley to do it. It didn't take too long because it's merely a variation on our game of fetch, only it involves grabbing a folded piece of daily journalism rather than a rubber ball. He repeated the action, I encouraged it, and it became one of Bentley's new skills. If I ask him to go out and get the paper, he will bring it back to me with tail-wagging joy. He knows he has found a new way to please me, and that makes him happy.

Are you coachable? Are you trainable? Are you willing and open to the idea of someone helping you move forward? Being coached can be the best way to break out of a rut if you are stuck. In fact, both words—*coach* and *train*—come from the world of transportation. A coach was originally a well-crafted carriage made in the town of Kosc, Croatia. Then it became the name for various vehicles, from a stagecoach to a bus. College students in the nineteenth century started calling their instructors a coach because they were carrying them forward into new realms of knowledge. So now a coach can refer to various types of instructors, but it still has that meaning of carrying you forward. Train means much the same thing, and it originally meant *pulling*. People would say a locomotive is pulling a train of railway cars down the track. So to be trained is to have someone pull you forward on the road to progress by helping you develop your skills. So the next time you are stuck, find yourself a coach or a trainer to activate your inner talents and get back on track.

What Would the Coach Do?

One CEO who has flourished by being coachable is Greg Flack, former CEO of Schwan's Food, a multi-billion dollar global company based in Marshall, Minnesota. Greg loved to play basketball in college. He enjoyed the sense of teamwork, the intense competition to win, and the confidence of being led by a good coach. In basketball, if you don't listen to the coach and play as a team, you are no longer truly competitive. You can't win. Greg also wanted to make a strong contribution to the team effort. He wanted to make a difference.

Greg carried those lessons with him more than twenty-six years ago when he went to work at Schwan's. His new coach was founder Marvin Schwan, who started out delivering ice cream goodies door to door, and the many successful assistant coaches who had grown the company for thirty-five years. Greg was pulled forward by Marvin in two ways. First, he kept rising in the company as the manager of various divisions in production and marketing, until he became CEO himself in 2008. Secondly, Greg learned important values from Marvin that were key ingredients in the Schwan's recipe for success. Like all business leaders, Marvin emphasized basic business principles, but he also wanted to make sure that all the employees were having fun and liked their work. You can't have a truly successful business unless the employees are enthusiastic and bring drive and a competitive spirit to what they do every day.

This human element is essential in relating well to customers, which brings up Marvin's great lesson about the purpose of the company. Sales. His original name for the company was Schwan's Sales Enterprises. That wasn't a very marketable name because people buy food, not sales, so they changed it to Schwan's Foods Company. But for many in the company, the old name never stopped being the true meaning of the company. Marvin always thought of Schwan's as a sales company.

As Greg worked his way up the ladder in his early years with Schwan's, he found that one division he managed had stalled. Things weren't working, growth wasn't happening, and morale was low. He knew he was in a position to make a difference, but how could he handle a complex problem he had never faced before? The answer is that he *had* seen the problem before, not on the job but on the football field. He dipped into his well of experience and retrieved his old lesson about the importance of teamwork, and that was the answer. He took a page out of his old playbook and began to lay out a clear vision so that everyone would be on the same page, so that they would work together with the same game plan. It was essential that everyone be aligned to the same objectives, processes, and goals.

He reformulated the team by putting the right people with the right talents in the right positions. Don't we want the tall guy under the basket? Finally, Greg made sure people acted like a team and communicated well with one another. Teamwork involves a lot of cooperation and mutual respect, and that means talking and listening to one another. Once everyone is working well together with a clear vision, the synergy kicks in and they move forward. In this case, the division experienced a turnaround and in one year had one of its best sales years ever. Greg's solution used the strengths he learned from his past successes and failures in competitive sports and beyond. He had become the division coach!

As a leader, Greg constantly retrieves the lessons that led him to the top. "I considered myself the 'Chief Talent Officer,'" said Greg, when discussing his approach. "I knew Schwan's could only get stronger by hiring talented people, and helping those talents grow."

He also keeps close to heart Marvin's emphasis on sales. "I am all too happy to follow Marvin's great ideas and vision for the company," he said, "because they still have the power to lead us to sustained growth in a competitive world." And Greg just loves that competition!

Although Greg has gone on to other interests today,

there is no doubt he will continue taking Marvin Schwan as his model and adding his own unique talents of influence and drive so that he and his employees will grow together, have fun, and form productive relationships with each other. Oh yes—and make sales!

How to Turn the Corner

Dave was the president of a small high-tech firm who found himself in the awkward position of inadvertently stalling his own company. He was a very talented individual, but some of his key talents lay dormant, and this caused a blind spot in his management style. He was a techie, and part of his job involved making sure his workers carried out all the various technical projects that his company relied on—setting up computer networks, installing company-wide Wi-Fi systems, and so forth. He loved to measure the results and collect data.

The problem was that Dave forgot he was dealing with living human beings, not hard drives filled with data. He became almost exclusively task-oriented while giving short shrift to the softer skills, such as being nice to people and encouraging them. But his obliviousness to his problem only made things worse and it affected the entire company. Other executives were frustrated. Many of his direct reports were at a loss themselves to know what to do, and the CEO was questioning whether he had hired the wrong guy.

He expressed all of this to me one day in his office and I suggested that if Dave was open to coaching and being personally accountable, we could sit down and have an open conversation. We did and this led to a live 360 review where I worked with Dave and picked the brains of seven of his colleagues to ascertain Dave's basic set of talents. I knew his leadership failure was a signal that he wasn't using all of his natural gifts. They needed to be coached out of him. The end result was that Dave realized he had gotten away from many of the things he was good at, and this undermined his leadership abilities and had a negative impact on the business. His core problem was that he needed to build better relationships with people.

I immediately gave Dave some specific actions that I knew would be helpful after reviewing the information we learned. For one thing, I got him out of his chair and away from his computer so he could walk around and talk with his colleagues. We are instinctively social animals, but that doesn't mean we socialize well unless we get out there and practice. He had gotten off track with people.

Dave responded well to getting back to unleashing his talents. He realized that he was ignoring his great talent for empathizing with people. Once he retrieved that talent and was coached on how to activate it, it made a big difference. He now walks around and talks to people, asks questions, listens more, shows great empathy, and uses his desire to grow as a model for others. He had forgotten what he knew and discovered some more talents in the coaching process, especially in the emotional intelligence area. His team says he is much more fun to be around because he has rediscovered the joy of practicing his many talents and seeing better results. Not to mention, the CEO is much happier.

After another month of success with the team and better results, we focused on a goal that Dave felt was key to making an even bigger impact in helping the sales team. We went through an exercise of listing his top five talents from the assessments, any areas that could derail him, three vital behaviors he wanted to influence with the team, and he began to look at this talent worksheet on a weekly basis. In fact, I suggested a scoring system so he could know how he was doing. After all, he loves numbers! The end result is that Dave is now back to building on his talent and succeeding in his role.

What Is The Difference between a Talent and a Skill?

Phil Mickelson is one of my favorite golfers because he is so incredibly gifted in the area of using his wedges around the green. I know he is a huge talent in general, but his short game has made him famous and allowed him to be one of the top golfers in the world. When I see his shots out of the sand trap, I just marvel at how he can do it. When he has just a few feet to land a ball so it can roll up to the cup, he has the unique ability to take a full swing with a 64-degree wedge and land it next to the cup. His ability is talent. His desire to practice this talent and hit all sorts of shots on a daily basis allows the talent to become exceptional. This becomes a skill. Skills are developed when we practice and become a student of whatever we are working at. Michael Jordan was amazing at hitting tough shots over opponents, but he practiced that over and over on the basketball court. Are you practicing your talent so it can become an exceptional skill?

Being Accountable

Back when I was ten years old, I loved going to the store to buy a toy truck or get some candy. I wanted to go much more often than my parents were willing to pay for.

One day Dad finally came out and gave me the basic wisdom of free enterprise, "If you really want to buy a fire truck so badly, go out and make some money."

Dad left for work that hot summer day and my mom left for a meeting, so I was home alone. My two brothers were busy with their friends, so I decided to follow my dad's advice and go out and earn some money. I knew my mom had been to the grocery store and picked up many frozen cans of lemonade, since this was a favorite in the Hiller household. I also knew that we lived near a golf course. My plan was to open a lemonade stand on the seventh hole and get rich. It was so hot outside, I was sure those thirsty golfers wouldn't mind paying a quarter for a glass of lemonade.

So, I started making batch after batch of lemonade and filled up all the pitchers we had. I loaded the filled pitchers onto my little red wagon, along with some paper cups, some ice cubes, and a little sign I made that said "Ice Cold Lemonade 25¢". Then I wheeled my mobile lemonade stand across our two neighbors' lawns until I reached the seventh hole. I parked my wagon next to the green and displayed my sign. It seemed that every golfer who walked by was delighted to see me, and most of them bought a glass. They were all so nice to me and one even gave me a tip. I had never heard of a tip, but I smiled and accepted it graciously! I sold so much lemonade that I ran out and had to run back home to make some more. What a hoot! I finally stopped when I ran out of frozen lemonade.

My parents arrived home around five o'clock and my dad immediately went to the refrigerator to get some lemonade. Of course, there was none to be found and he yelled over to my mom, "Dorothy, where the heck is all the lemonade? I'm thirsty." She walked over and looked with disbelief that all ten cans were gone.

I had been watching this episode the whole time, cringing and trying to stay out of sight. My dad yelled for me and said, "Robby, what happened to all the lemonade?"

I stood up and said, "You told me I needed to earn some money for my fire truck, so I did just that this afternoon." I told them what I did and finally a big smile broke over his face and my mom started laughing. I thought this was a good sign.

Dad then said, "Good going, now we are going to learn about cost of goods sold so you can repay your mother!"

That's when I was introduced to the concept of business expenses and the meaning of accountability.

When I think back to this and other things in my life, it was evident that I liked business and was always looking for a way to make things better. I found some thirsty golfers who loved having an ice cold lemonade. I found a need and provided a solution. This became a pattern over my years growing up.

Pay Attention To Your Passion!

When you were a kid, what was your passion or natural inclination? What did you love to do back when you had enough time to do anything you wanted? You may want to retrieve some of your lost talents from childhood, because it could make a big difference in how you perform as a leader today.

The founder of Twitter, Jack Dorsey, is a total introvert. As a youngster he used to play with computers and write software programs for fun. Another hobby was listening to police chatter on the dispatch channel. He noticed they spoke in a code of sorts, shortened words, phrases, or initials that meant something to all the insiders. This gave him the idea of putting together short communication bursts now known across the world as "tweets." This was his way of connecting without having to be face to face, which he preferred because of his shyness. His talents became unleashed and his being an introvert and enjoying reading and thinking has made a profound impact on how we communicate today. Are you retrieving your talents, practicing, and developing so you can make the impact that you are destined to make?

Josh Chamberlain: A Leader Who Saved America

The ongoing task of every great leader is to go forward.

We live in a world that is constantly changing, so if you don't keep up with it you will be left behind in various ways. If Bentley didn't learn any new tricks, people might get bored and ignore him. Businesses that don't innovate lose revenue when some other company that's really moving takes the lead. And in war, getting stuck in the field can mean death, and sometimes the fate of the nation hangs in the balance.

During the Civil War, one talented leader at a single skirmish, in a single battle, may have changed the course of the entire war. His actions, therefore, may have changed the path of the United States as the Land of the Free.

Lieutenant Colonel Josh Chamberlain was leading the 20th Maine Infantry on Little Round Top at the battle of Gettysburg, Pennsylvania. Confederate General Robert E. Lee had made his deepest incursion into Union territory, and his powerful offensive was on the version of breaking the Union forces in two, whereby his next move would be to swing down to the east and capture Washington, D.C.

The Confederates were gaining much ground during the first day of the battle, and Union forces were driven back to defensive positions. Lee figured the weakest point was the far left flank of the Union defensive line, right at a hill called Little Round Top. So on the second day of the battle, he sent a strong force led by the 15th Alabama Infantry charging up the hill.

The soldiers from Maine on top of the hill fended off the Confederates almost to a standstill, but then they ran out of ammunition.

Any trained military commander in his right mind would have realized that all hope was lost and the time had come to flee. But Lieutenant Colonel Chamberlain was not a military man. He had no idea about the proper military strategy. He was a professor. He was an academic who had taught himself to read and write Classical Greek.

He knew more about calculus than canons.

He had joined the war to save the American way of life, and turning around and fleeing was not a possibility. In his mind, a good leader always pushes forward. He knew his men were out of bullets, but they still had their bayonets. Chamberlain's talent was logic. He retrieved the bookish common sense that had been trained into him, and did the only logical thing. He ordered a bayonet charge, something that was extremely rare during the early era of modern warfare. His men were trained to obey, and they were trained to fight.

The brave soldiers from Maine charged down the hill with bayonets as their only weapons. The unorthodox attack threw the confederates off guard. Then the far left end of the bayonet charge swung over and up like a wheel, capturing what was left of the 15th Alabama Infantry and taking them prisoner. From that moment forward, the tide of the battle changed. Some historians credit Chamberlain with saving the battle and the United States itself. He was awarded the Congressional Medal of Honor for his gallantry in action.

You don't have to fight in a war to demonstrate the same creative leadership as Lieutenant Colonel Chamberlain. At a moment of desperation when the Union was stuck, he put it back on track by relying on his inherent talent of clear thinking, and his practical skills of applied logic.

An Extraordinary Sales Executive

A number of years ago I met an extraordinary sales leader while I was consulting with American Medical Systems. Ric worked for AMS, but was eventually hired by CEO Mark to head up sales for a faltering medical device company, Conceptus Medical Inc. out in Mountain View, California. As in so many cases where sales are not going up, Ric quickly discovered that the current sales force was comprised of people whose talents weren't a good fit for the product. They had been successful cardiovascular or orthopedic med device reps, pretty standard stuff in the medical device world. The problem was that they didn't necessarily have the skills to sell *innovative* technology to a new target market of OBGYNs, because Conceptus produced a device that enabled permanent birth control in a fifteen-minute office procedure. It was revolutionary.

Ric saw that a revamp of talent had to be made if there was going to be positive change. So he recruited great new sales reps that knew how to sell innovative products. One of the most amazing talents that Ric had was his ability to conceptualize solutions to a problem by being able to envision and analyze the big picture. We refer to that skill in our assessment as *theoretical problem solving*. He could quickly see an issue, figure it out, and come up with various solutions.

Ric's other incredible talents were in the people category. He knew how to be sensitive toward others and display genuine empathy. He understood that everyone has different motivational needs. Finally, his ability to engage in proactive thinking helped him be personally accountable. Ric was able to unleash his talents and the CEO, Mark, had the foresight to encourage and recognize these talents. The two of them made change fun and developed a great culture. They both were visionaries.

In the early stages of a company, you need an extraordinary sales leader who can see things others can't see. He or she needs to inspire, be highly empathetic when a sales team is plowing new ground, and have the ability to make things happen with creative solutions. Ric had all the abilities, and Conceptus grew from a small, struggling $6 million company to making roughly $141 million in annual revenue in five years.

His uncanny ability to connect with people and inspire them made him an exemplary leader. The other qualities I will mention are Ric's commitment to being coachable and his desire to develop people. I would sit by his desk when I visited the corporate office and listen to how he handled the sales leader who had an issue or the salesperson who was all excited about a success they had just experienced. He listened, encouraged them, and used his talents to solve any issues at hand. And why? All through my time working with Ric and the team, he constantly tried to improve himself, as he was coachable and accountable to do what he said he would do. And he did. A large company, Bayer, recently paid over $1 billion for the business that at one time was headed for the graveyard.

Two Keys to Leadership: Personal Accountability and Coachability

My parents taught me about the importance of accountability, and it is a gift I carry with me today. They emphasized taking personal responsibility for my actions—whether good or bad—as well as for my inactions, when I chose to do nothing. They gave me an opportunity to demonstrate my accountability every time they gave me advice on what I should do. Was I going to heed their advice or not? They rubbed this in with their constant mantra: "Listen to what your mom and dad have to say." This is called coaching!

At the time, I rebelled every so often, but the lesson did not fail. I remembered from my failures and learned to be accountable. More important, I gradually became more coachable, and by the time I was working at Xerox, they truly helped make me a leader. If I did not hit my sales numbers each month, it was up to me and no one else. If I chose to heed all the great training I received on a constant basis, I found my results got better and better.

Yes, I was slow to become susceptible to coaching, but my experience at Xerox took care of that with a public form of accountability that everyone in the company could see. I couldn't stand being at the bottom of the sales rankings chart! So I listened, took coaching at every opportunity. Coachability and being personally accountable changed my life.

Activating My Gifts and Talents Exercise: Your Talents

1- To activate your gifts, look back at the two exercises in chapter 1 and 2 and review your discoveries in the list you have already completed.

2- What are your two top motivating values from Chapter 2?

3- Complete the following exercise and focus on your top five to seven talents. (If you want to complete the scientific assessment, see our website for more information.)

Talent Exercise

Here are twenty-three talents that you can rate yourself on, with 10 being the highest and 1 the lowest score. Choose your top five by circling those below and ask someone else who knows you if they agree. Ask yourself how often you can focus and find more ways to use these talents!

TALENT	YOUR SELF SCORING (1-10)
1. Accountability for Others	
2. Conceptual Thinking	
3. Conflict Management	
4. Continuous Learning	
5. Customer Focus	
6. Decision Making	
7. Developing Others	
8. Diplomacy and Tact	
9. Empathetic Outlook	
10. Flexibility	
11. Goal Achievement	
12. Influencing Others	
13. Interpersonal Skills	
14. Leading Others	
15. Personal Accountability	
16. Objective Listening	
17. Planning and Organization	
18. Problem Solving	
19. Resiliency	
20. Results Orientation	
21. Self-Management	
22. Self-Starting Ability	
23. Teamwork	

Paw Prints to Remember

🐾 Our talents allow us to make progress when we retrieve, practice, and develop each one.

🐾 We are at our best when we are coachable and accountable in the process of developing our talents into exceptional skills.

🐾 You can change and get better when you return to the basics of knowing your talents and start focusing on these strengths. Coaching will rapidly speed up your success. Bentley says, "Call me!"

🐾 Remembering your passion as a kid can be a way to travel back in the past to unleash your gifts to solve today's problems. Take a moment and do so!

🐾 If Josh Chamberlain can defeat a division with no bullets in his guns, you can overcome any obstacle in your way with your own personal natural resources—your talents!

CHAPTER 4

DON'T LET IT BOTHER YOU; SHAKE IT OFF! PICK UP YOUR POOP!

Shake It Off, Bentley!

Bentley has supreme confidence in his talents and abilities, so when things don't go his way, he doesn't get all bent out of shape. He just shakes it off and continues on his merry way. This happened the other day when we visited our favorite upscale hamburger place, the Gold Nugget. We sat in the outdoor dining area so Bentley could join us, and as we wound our way through all the tables, Bentley greeted the diners in his usual fashion. Nearly everyone turned and smiled at our lovable British lab. It was almost comical. A table of men were laughing and drinking beer, and as soon as we walked by, they all stopped their conversation and got up to see Bentley. These men were in the middle of telling stories, and I bet they would have kept on talking if their wives walked up to them! But they fell under the spell of Bentley's magic.

But some people are immune to his charms. On occasion we will find a person who is not fond of animals and Bentley's smiles are returned with a scowl. We have to cut this unwanted greeting short with a deep-voiced command for Bentley to back off. His immediate response is to put his head down with his ears back since he knows he has crossed the line. But Bentley doesn't sulk for very long. He bounces back almost instantly to his genuine lovable self. But when we leave, he is careful to avoid showing the same friendliness to the person who was wary of him. Bentley does not hold a grudge. He simply shakes it off, forgives himself, accepts reality, and goes back to being Bentley.

Obstacles Require a Positive Attitude

We can learn a lot about becoming a successful leader from Bentley's flexible attitude when everything doesn't happen perfectly. If we get thrown off track by occasional obstacles, we can lose our way and forget who we truly are. We become oblivious to our larger purpose and forsake happiness and success. When something unexpected happens, we must deal with it, and then get on with things. Shake it off, and return to your core values and activities.

There are two basic types of obstacles that can derail us from the path of success. The first category contains those things that simply happen to us, things that are thrust upon us that we cannot control. We may be thrown off course by the economy, natural disasters, or disease. A car could hit us while we are at a stop sign, or a new competitor could come out of nowhere and cause havoc to our business. We wonder, "Why does this have to happen to me?"

The second category contains self-inflicted problems

that we cause by our decisions, actions, or inaction. When things don't turn out well because we have made a mistake, we can veer off our path to success, plus we can cause pain, heartache, and discomfort to others.

In both areas, we must learn to respond to these negative events in healthy ways. If we let the circumstances bring us down, we become immobilized and ineffective. We must try to be like Bentley and shake things off the best we can, even if we must endure unpleasantness. A good leader always keeps moving forward!

I have had many of these life events fall upon me. Eight years ago, I went for my yearly physical and everything turned out great—except for the prostate screening. My numbers on the PSA test skyrocketed and I was immediately sent to a urologist who did a biopsy. The test results were not good and they discovered I had the dreaded "Big C": cancer. The doctor recommended immediate surgery.

It seems as though almost everyone has been affected by cancer in some way, directly or indirectly. You either have had it or you know someone who has discovered the dreaded disease and is taking radiation or chemo. My mom lost her life to breast cancer after a courageous ten-year battle. I had seen what pain and suffering she had gone through, and I braced myself for the unknown.

I responded to this devastating news by gathering a support team of good friends, my pastor, and my wife Pam. Since I had worked in the medical device field, I picked the brains of former colleagues and clients who were in the know about what treatment options were available. I discovered a new procedure performed by a robot that gave patients a much better chance for avoiding nerve damage during the operation because it could "see" everything ten times more clearly. The procedure uses the da Vinci robotic machine. After seeing five different urologists, I found one in Minneapolis who was using the da Vinci robotic machine, and I would be patient number thirty.

It was tempting to wallow in self-pity and ask "Why me?" but I did not want to go to that dark place because it zapped my energy. Instead, I thrived on hope and optimism rather than fear by taking action to find the best treatment options, plus I was lifted up by the support and prayers of many people. Thankfully, the procedure was a total success and I am cancer free eight years later. Today, the da Vinci robotic machine is used routinely in various types of surgeries.

It is fun to see Bentley jump out of the lake dripping wet, and then shake wildly till he is dry.

But his simple instinctive behavior is also a profound lesson in dealing with our problems. We cannot whimper helplessly at our plight; rather we should just let go the best way we know how, and continue on as cheerfully and positively as we can. But what happens when this isn't so easy to do? Can we learn to more effectively deal with adversity in positive ways? The answer is yes. Emotional intelligence is a key area that impacts all of us and the good news is that our EQ can be improved!

Emotional Intelligence

Leadership begins with becoming aware of your inner talents, but long-range success also requires being acquainted with your emotions. Western civilization has long praised the value of reason over feelings, and philosophers often refer to man as the "rational animal." But psychologists (and advertisers!) have known for years that people are really driven by their emotions. People crave positive emotions like joy, love, and excitement, and we try to avoid negative emotions such as fear, pain, and worry. Since emotions are so primal and instinctual within us, we have to become familiar with them if we have any hope of trying to control them. It is also important to understand emotions when dealing with other people—especially your employees and customers!

The ability to understand and deal with your emotions is called your *emotional intelligence*, a term popularized by Daniel Goleman, who wrote a book of the same name. In contrast to your cognitive abilities, your so-called "IQ," researchers now emphasize your emotional intelligence with a corresponding label—your "EQ." While your IQ is fairly stable throughout your life, your EQ can increase the more you work at it. A high EQ is also more correlated to success than a high IQ. Goleman found that workers with a high EQ are 127 times more productive than those with low EQ. He concluded that the key differentiator between star performers and average performers is EQ. You will make better decisions when you improve your EQ. Therefore, it is important to understand yourself and others in terms of the emotions that inspire them, motivate them, and at times—obstruct them. Empathy is an essential instrument in the tool kit of all executives.

Negative emotions have the power to linger in you and sabotage your success. Guilt, fear, regret, and similar feelings can persist as a heavy burden that weighs down your talents. Perhaps you have had a conflict with a co-worker, and your feelings of blame and revenge dominate your mind to the point where you no long function effectively at work. Maybe you made a big mistake at work and you can't get over it. A high EQ means you have the ability to recognize such garbage for what it is, and then shake it off and get on with your work. Perhaps a more apt metaphor here is to scoop up your poop and flush it away.

Emotions are also contagious. Research shows that one low EQ person in a group who is letting his emotions negatively influence his decisions will bring down the entire group's EQ. Such a person can undercut the morale of an entire office. When it comes to dysfunctional emotions, one bad apple can spoil the whole bunch. However, a good leader with a high EQ can spot that problem and take steps to restore a better attitude and create a safe and sane workplace. If you know of someone who seems to be negative most of the time, talk to him or her about the impact this has on the team and get them back to reviewing the first three chapters of this book. They obviously don't know themselves and most likely struggle with being who they are.

There are five core areas that make up EQ: self-awareness, self-regulation, motivation, empathy, and social skills. It is amazing to me as a consultant to see how a low score in one of those areas impacts the performance of a leader. One of the most common for executives is low self-awareness. When they complete our EQ assessment and we review the results with the leader, it becomes obvious what areas need work and how they can improve with some fairly simple strategies. In most cases, a leader can improve in this area in a few weeks by being more aware of how they are feeling about their daily interactions with people and how the other people might be feeling. It isn't that big of a leap to genuinely ask someone how they feel about a potential solution, issue, or how their job is going.

As we know from watching Bentley in action, when you listen and have a positive cheery attitude, it can brighten up the whole workplace, and raise the EQ of an entire group.

CEO with High EQ: Rhoda Olsen of Great Clips Inc.

Emotional intelligence is a necessity for Rhoda Olsen, the

CEO of Great Clips, a highly successful Minneapolis-based franchisor of hair salons. She needs to empathize with 1,200 franchisees to persuade them to align with the company's objectives. Great Clips does not operate any corporate salons, so any testing of new designs or processes needs to be a true collaboration because it works best when the franchisees willingly cooperate. Using a heavy hand promotes conflict. That's why Olsen places a high priority on building relationships with franchisees, listening to their concerns, and always admitting mistakes without dwelling on who is to blame. At the same time she tries to coach her corporate staff to adopt a similar empathetic attitude toward franchisees to prevent a needless rise in negative emotions. Olsen shared a story about how shaking off a major mistake and starting over allowed the company to introduce a new salon design.

Many years ago we decided we really needed a new salon design, so a group of corporate staff members and a few franchisees got together and came up with a bold new design to totally change the way the salons looked. We had not changed our look for fifteen or sixteen years, and in the meantime our market had become much more competitive. The dynamic had changed.

So we went through this process and we got a little bit off track. The design they came up with was not consistent with our brand and it was too expensive. The franchisees were up in arms, and so we had to regroup. It was a fairly contentious situation because it was expensive and there was not a lot of support for it.

Add to this the fact that new franchisees are very fearful. And people when they are afraid do not always behave well. They are afraid because they have invested their life savings, they have invested their child's college fund— and then things are not going well. They are used to being in control and they were very successful in their prior business. They cannot quite shake this off. You need to just be there and listen. It became a very contentious and emotional situation.

Finally I sat down with my VP in charge of the process and I said, "We have backed everyone into a corner. We are all in our defensive positions. We need to figure out how to go forward in a positive way. We just aren't where we need to be, so we are going to back up and start over."

And it is really funny—we used those words consistently from that point forward: "We are going to back up and start over." It didn't get defensive, it did not blame anyone, it was sort of like shaking it off. We just weren't where we needed to be, so we just backed up started all over. We knew there had to be a salon design that everyone was excited about, and it didn't make sense for us to go forward until everyone was on board. Once people are in a negative frame of mind, your ability to influence them is rather limited.

Rhoda's approach worked and she is admired as one of the finest CEOs in the country. Great Clips was able to get a broad consensus from its franchisees for a new design that was affordable and that strengthened the brand.

To Err Is Human, to Forgive Divine—and Scientifically Proven!

When modern science agrees with the ancient wisdom of the world's great religions, then we know we have a truth we can rely on. They agree that forgiveness is good for you. It just so happens that showing mercy and compassion as a response to injustice is one of the best ways to "shake things off" and get moving again on your path to leadership. The opposite approach is to stubbornly hold a grudge until you can wield revenge. It is certainly natural to desire payback and to harbor resentment when you are wronged. But that scenario is one of the strongest emotional obstacles to the ultimate productive activity of manifesting your innate gifts and talents. Look at all of the obsessive feuds that take place in workplaces, and between various groups around the nation and the world. The "Hatfield and McCoy" mindset is instinctual and per-vasive—but it is also destructive for both sides.

In 1985 researchers at the University of Wisconsin at Madison set up experiments to determine whether for-giveness is actually good for your emotional health. They examined ancient religious texts to try to define the con-cept of forgiveness, looking at literature from Hebrew, Confucian, Buddhist, Christian, Muslim, and Hindu sourc-es. They discovered that a common theme of the virtue of showing mercy in the face of wrongdoing did not in-clude condoning the unjust action; justice was still on the agenda. The difference is an emotional release toward the person who committed the act—and a correspond-ing release of resentment in the injured person, the one who suffered the injustice. They did not excuse the unjust action; they simply changed their emotional response to it by distinguishing between the act and the person who committed it.

The researchers conducted randomized clinical trials using people who had been unjustly wronged in various ways—women who were emotionally abused, young and old people who had been hurt by other family mem-bers, incest survivors, drug addicts in recovery, cardiac patients filled with anger, crime victims, etc. The stud-ies overwhelmingly showed that people who practiced forgiveness showed remarkable improvement in their emotional health. They were better able to "shake things off" and get on with their lives. Even the incest victims showed positive results a year after the study was over, and some escaped debilitating depression.

Science has proved what many have known for centuries. Granting forgiveness actually bolsters our emotional health and provides a way of healing when we are treated unjustly. This is great news for all of us who may be carrying this burden and it is so easy to do! The study then devised a pathway to help people who willingly choose to forgive. That pathway is described in the book *Forgiveness Is a Choice*, written by Robert D. Enright and published by the American Psychological Association. The book outlines twenty guideposts in the forgiveness process that can be boiled down to three *steps:*

1- Self-reflection. The person who has been wronged looks at what the injustice has done to his or her emotions. Do you feel anger, hatred, depression, resentment, or other negative emotions? Do you want to stop feeling bad?

2- Resolution. The motivation to feel better prompts the decision to forgive, while keeping in mind that the offering of mercy does not condone or justify the harmful action.

3- Action and renewal. The act of showing mercy replaces the stubborn old mindset with a new and healthier perspective. By showing empathy and compassion, the forgiver sees the unjust person in a new way. This new attitude is rewarded with healthier emotions and the renewed ability to move forward with your life.

The Power of Being Forgiven and Self-Forgiveness: CEO Jay Coughlan of XRS

What happens when a top executive commits a tragic crime? In the case of Jay Coughlan, the power of forgiveness made all of the difference in his ability to rebound and soar as a leader. Coughlan had been rising through the ranks of St. Paul-based Lawson Software for years and had found success as the leader of its health care division, but one day he made a terrible mistake.

During his adult years his father had become his best friend. The two of them went on a hunting trip together, and one evening they had too much to drink at a bar. Jay attempted to drive home drunk, but he missed a turn, and the car left the road and crashed. Jay awoke in a hospital severely injured. He soon entered a personal hell when he discovered that his father had died in the crash, and that he was facing felony charges. He had killed his father and now he was going to jail. What had he done? What would he do now?

That's when he discovered the power of receiving forgiveness from others. He soon learned that his wife forgave him, his mother forgave him, his friends forgave him, and his employer forgave him. No one condoned his actions, but they separated the actions from the person and showed him compassion. But how could Jay ever forgive himself for his horrible deed? The breakthrough came when he took that maxim to heart that forgiveness was divine, and he came to the realization that even God forgave him. Just as in the third step of forgiveness listed above, Jay looked at himself with new eyes and began living life with a new attitude. He learned to forgive himself.

Prior to my accident I was a very aggressive and arrogant individual. I would have run you over very easily. And now there was a bigger calling, there was a bigger purpose. My realization of forgiveness gave me a sense of serving a larger purpose than myself. I did not know it at the time, but probably the biggest thing it did for me was humility. Now I have more of a servant attitude.

There were a lot of reasons I could have given up when I was in jail. My religious experience and sense of forgiveness gave me patience and peace, and it allowed me to sleep. It allowed me to keep things in a proper perspective. And doing that, it allowed me to come in and live another day, another episode. Whereas if you get too hung up on worry, it freezes you. It ultimately leads you to depression. Thanks to forgiveness, I did not linger on that guilt trip.

Adversity is a relative thing; what seems hard to me might seem light to you. It doesn't matter, it still seems hard to me. So where is your foundation to deal with this issue? If your foundation is only your work, you are really in trouble when it goes bad. Or if your whole identity is just in work, you are going to be in trouble when it goes bad. Or you are going to be inflated disproportionately if it goes well.

Friends, family, and faith became the offset to help me get through any kinds of issues. So for me it's that foundational question, where do you go when things go bad? Where do you go when things are good? You remain humble.

I miss my dad to this day. The only person who is hurt when you're not giving forgiveness is yourself. I believe you can forgive but not forget. There are business people that I do not trust and I would not work with them again. I have forgiven them. I can still go have lunch with them; they are not bad people. It was just a circumstance we were in, but I do not forget. So in my dad's situation, I have been forgiven, but I do not forget.

But if you can have that inner peace, it allows you to go on confidently with energy, which you are going to need.

Because of the tremendous support Jay received from everyone, he was given a reduced sentence and was allowed to work part of each day and return to jail at night. His dedication to his job and his humbler attitude prompted him to handle assignments and take on responsibilities far beyond his job title. Things were set right when he was named president and CEO. He served in that position for five years. Jay is now the CEO of another high-tech company, XRS. Oh yes, Jay, Bentley is so proud of you!

So Shake It Off!

We are highly gifted but emotional creatures who need to maintain balance to move forward as leaders. We must be constantly aware of when our activities are being stifled by disruptive emotions. It may be trivial bickering with a co-worker or a profound personal tragedy that gives rise to obstructive emotions. No matter what the cause, our best response is to face reality without undue worry or obsession, and get on with it. Shake it off!

Emotional intelligence can help us stay on our path, and it is essential when dealing with others. Learn to foresee situations the way Rhoda Olsen does, to circumvent defensiveness in others. Building high EQ relationships will help your business succeed. At the same time, keep a proper humble attitude toward your work, following the example of Jay Coughlan. It is easier to place our various situations in proper perspective when we see the bigger picture, and that can remove unneeded drama from the workplace. And always keep in mind the healing power of forgiveness!

Everyone I know has experienced an argument with a spouse, boss, co-worker, or good friend at some time. We all worry about too much and will be more effective when we do what Bentley does when he comes out of the water: shake it off!

Understanding My Gifts: EQ Exercise

EQ is the most important part of leveraging or de-leveraging your talent! Of the five key areas of EQ— self-awareness, self-regulation, motivation, empathy, and social skills—which ones might be holding you back? Here are some questions to ask yourself that may be of help. Score yourself on a 1-10 scale with 10 being the best score.

1- Self-Awareness. How self-aware are you of your own moods, emotions, drives, and those of others?

2- Self-Regulation. When something happens out of the blue that you really don't like, to what extent does that send you to the moon? Do you suspend judgment first or usually judge and then get the information? How long does it take for you to go from "red" to "clear?

3- Motivation. To what extent do you work for reasons beyond money or status, but just for the passion of achieving something meaningful with persistence?

4- Empathy. How well do you really understand the emotional make-up of other people?

5- Social Skills. How good are you at developing and building strong relationships with others and creating networks?

Paw Prints to Remember

🐾 Shaking it off. Science and experience from others say this is a no-brainer, but we can have difficulty doing it. Try it out by forgiving yourself for something you have done and begin to unblock those areas that may be holding you back.

🐾 Email or call someone that you have unfinished business with today and just begin a conversation. Simple!

🐾 Pick up your poop! One of the highest forms of integrity is simply saying I am sorry. Who needs to hear this from you?

🐾 Forgiveness is a conscious decision. It does not mean forgetting nor does it mean you always have to be a person's best friend. But it does free you to unleash your talents and move on in a healthy and productive way.

🐾 Take personal responsibility and experience forgiveness. It is your path to freedom.

CHAPTER 5

BE A GUIDE DOG!
THE JOY OF BRINGING OTHERS ALONG

Where's The Boat, Bentley?

The next best thing to having a home on beautiful Lake Minnetonka is keeping a boat there. One of our favorite ways to become totally refreshed is to take a one or two hour vacation out on the boat. A few years ago, we decided to rent a slip that has a full cover for our boat so we wouldn't have the hassle of always taking the boat cover off and putting it back on again after our little cruise on the lake.

Last spring I drove out to see the boat and brought Bentley with me, since he loves going out on the lake. After a long winter with much snow, we couldn't wait to smell the water and hear the waves. We drove up to the long line of slips with canopies and Bentley bolted out of the car. He dashed over to the small planks that lead out to a long row of boats, and immediately went to our boat slip and waited for me.

I found it mind-boggling that Bentley remembered where we parked the boat last October! He knows the exact location where we left off and guides me back to it. He performs the same service when visitors come boating with us; he shows them exactly where they need to go to start having fun.

Once again Bentley has demonstrated a natural talent that all leaders need to emulate, how to guide people.

Leaders Must Be Guides

Learning to guide others is the flip side of being coachable. Sometimes you need help tapping into your talents and finding the right position to perform your best. The same is true for your employees. They often need your help to shine, so you need to learn to be like Bentley. Your job is to guide people when they need it.

Guiding people is not the same as bossing them around. Think of it in terms of emotional intelligence. Do you want to fill people with fear, frustration, and resentment because they are always told what to do? Or do you want to engage them willingly in the team effort, give them a sense of purpose they can believe in, and perform with confidence? To be a good guide, you need a high EQ.

Emotional intelligence is especially important when you endeavor to coach the highest leaders in the land. The Reverend Billy Graham displayed that skill especially well as a coach to every U.S. president from Dwight Eisenhower to George W. Bush. Graham never told any of these men what to do, but he helped them all become better leaders by encouraging them to tap into their inner strengths through prayer, contemplation, and discussion.

Each president is surrounded by people urging him to make this decision or that decision, waving results from opinion polls or think tanks to support their goals, and pointing out the political consequences of each move. Graham understood that each president was the center of an emotional storm, and that a sense of peace and universal brotherhood is necessary to make the best decisions. After all, presidential decisions have the power to affect many millions of people.

So in 1957 when President Eisenhower was considering whether to send federal troops to Arkansas to end racial segregation in schools, he called for his coach, Billy Graham. With Graham's help, Eisenhower found the strength to defy the political naysayers and sent the 101st Airborne Division of the U.S. Army to escort nine African American students into their high school in Little Rock.

Graham followed up on this effort when he brought his crusade to Arkansas the following year, and refused to allow the local organizers to segregate the audience. This had a big impact on a 12-year-old boy attending the event, William Jefferson Clinton. Years later President Clinton would seek Graham for some coaching of his own.

Similarly, when President George H. W. Bush was deliberating on whether to launch the Gulf War in 1991, he, too, sought out Billy Graham for coaching and inspiration. And so it was with Lyndon Johnson, Richard Nixon, Gerald Ford, Ronald Reagan, and George W. Bush. They all realized that emotional and spiritual strength would help them make better decisions.

But how do you dare coach the highest office holder in the land? What is Billy Graham's secret? The answer is that he approached each president with a sense of humility. He was not out for personal gain or political favors; he just wanted each president to perform better for the sake of the nation. He was not out to boss them around. In this way Billy Graham unleashed his talents and had an impact on the entire world.

Great coaches are followed when they show genuine love and respect for people, share their vision, and then help people be more successful. A great way to help guide people is to ask thoughtful questions, and that is one of the reasons for Billy Graham's success. He challenged people with great questions. He knows who is he is, he knows his talents, and he is known today as an inspiring guide to millions around the world.

Research Confirms the Need for Successful Guide Dogs!

If more leaders would follow these simple, yet profound principles to being a guide and coach to others, the following research would be far different. Most leaders struggle and fall short when it comes to coaching. The sad fact is that most companies are not successful in keeping their employees engaged in their jobs. It's just the opposite. In a 2013 Gallup Poll on the topic, Gallup CEO Jim Clifton said, "Managers from hell are creating active disengagement costing the U.S. an estimated $450 to $550 billion annually." The poll's shocking results said that 70 million out of roughly 100 million working people in the United States are either disengaged or not really coming to work fully engaged. This tremendous disengagement saps the creativity of people and adds stress to nearly everyone." The attitude is summed up in the title of my colleague Terri Kabachnick's book, *I Quit But Forgot to Tell You!*

You shouldn't have to work in an environment where people are merely present and not engaged. **You can help be an agent of change**. If you want to make a real difference in whatever you are doing, you must win the hearts and minds of your people. Disengagement is the ultimate emotional washout in the workplace: people just don't care.

The Way Out of Disengagement—Successful Guide Dog Tips

I have spent the last eighteen years working with leaders and their teams to improve results and it is so rewarding to see positive change come from following the four steps outlined in the previous chapters.

This next step in being an effective guide dog is to have others truly identify with the vision of what you are doing and then be genuinely concerned about bringing them along on the journey. You must care about *their* success—along with the success of the business. When you are focused on your own success, you won't be as successful or experience the joy of helping others. So here are some general guide dog tips!

Put the right talent in the right job the first time.

It is proven that profits rise when we do the above and become a successful coach.

Communicate the vision with enthusiasm and engage people.

Truly care for other people and find out what motivates them.

WCCO Sports Announcer Mike Max on Coaching

My favorite sports announcer is Mike Max. He is one of the most giving people you will meet and one of the busiest. We sat down to talk late one night after his WCCO radio program, *Sports to the Max*. Mike is considered by many the heir apparent to one of America's best sportswriters, who is now ninety-three years young, Sid Hartman of the *Minneapolis Star Tribune*. In his sports reports on radio and television, Mike reveals a zeal to find out what makes people tick. He told me one of the greatest "guide dog" leaders he ever met was former head coach of the Minnesota Vikings, Bud Grant.

One indication that Bud Grant is a great leader is that the players respected him. Back when he was head coach, there was no sign that reserved his parking spot at Winter Park. Everyone knew it was Bud Grant's spot. He did not have to tell anybody he was the boss; everybody knew that.

At a speech recently someone asked Bud whether he would be motivated by coaching modern-day athletes. He said, "Stop. It is not the players' job to motivate me. It is my job to figure out how to motivate the players. It is not the players' job to try to please me. It is my job to figure out what motivates them. And it always will be."

The opposite of that is, "It's my way or the highway." I am going to put your square peg in a round hole and you better like it. And you have no say in it. This is not a partnership, and those guys are never going to play for you. The team leaders are going to rebel and that is going to filter down to the other players. So Bud said, "I have to win over the players, the players do not have to win over me."

If he is trying to win them over and they are trying to win him over, then you really have something. You have a partnership. But some coaches will overthink it or they try to make themselves the hero. That's why a new coach makes such a difference coming in to teams of equal talent.

Most of the time the new coaches are not necessarily great leaders. That is far more common than the other. Part of the reason is because the players are not going to blame themselves. So when things go wrong, the players blame the coaches, and the coaches blame the players. Every time. It is human nature. It is hardwired. You don't want to look into the mirror and admit your own faults—and you compound that when there is a coach that they cannot trust. Or who they think has ulterior motives.

And if the leaders of that team figure that out about that coach, it is over. If the players and the team did not trust that coach, it is over. Fire him now, because it is done.

I think this is where sports and business are the same. If you don't believe in your culture or your leadership, you're going to have all kinds of conversations around the coffee pot that are not productive.

When you walk into a room and know what motivates each person, isn't it easier to guide the conversations and get things done? It is about being outwardly focused and helping others move the ball forward. Maybe it is time to throw the ball out there, more like what we do with Bentley! Bentley always brings back the ball to us with his tail going back and forth and eager for the next challenge. I think you will find the same to be true when you do this for others!

Paul Harmel, CEO of Lifetouch

If you have a child who has had a school picture taken, it was most likely done by Lifetouch. When our son Ryan graduated from high school a few years ago, my wife Pam displayed all the pictures from Lifetouch showing his kindergarten picture up through his senior year. Do you remember yours? As one looks back at the changes, memories of each year certainly flood a parent's mind. But it is not just us parents. Ryan sat and laughed in disbelief as he looked at images of his own awkward stages. There is nothing quite like a picture that captures a point in time because our lives are a collection of memories.

This is the exact emotional connection that Lifetouch aims for, and it is also ingrained in the corporate culture.

CEO Paul Harmel is full of warmth and has a passion for touching lives through professional photography. Paul knows this ever so well, and that is why he changed the name of the company to Lifetouch. When you first meet Paul, you would never guess that thirty-six years ago he used to be the comptroller of Lifetouch, the world's largest employee-owned photography company. He is one of the more engaging finance people you will ever meet! This people-oriented culture is the driving force behind the Minneapolis-based company that was struggling to meet its bills thirty-six years ago, and makes over $1.2 billion in revenue today.

One of the ways I help employees to stay engaged is to serve as a mentor by asking people questions about how they feel about things. I think most people know in their emotions when there is a conflict with how they are spending their career. So I ask, "What are your guts telling you?"

If they ask me what they should do, I don't think I should be the judge. They need to come to their conclusion themselves of what is right for them or what is wrong for them. So I ask them some questions. "How do you feel when you say this? How do you feel when you think about that? How do you feel?" These questions lead back to their own thinking and feeling, because most of the time people are confused. It is not just logic, it is emotions, and they have not sorted it out. So I try to help them sort it out and add some logic and practicality to it. They come back and say, "Yeah, I have these butterflies in my stomach" or something like that.

Of course when you are in a managing situation, it is wrong to be too concerned about their feelings, because you have to be brutally honest sometimes. One of the biggest mistakes that a lot of managers make is being too nice instead of being direct and honest. You are not doing that person any favors, because how can they change and/or improve if they do not have the truth? "The truth will set you free." So as a manager you are really responsible to speak truth. Now you can do it the Attila the Hun way or you can do it in a more humane way. It does not mean you have no empathy or compassion for somebody. I have great angst over it, but it is the right thing to do.

One way that I help guide younger employees is by telling them a story of an experience during my early days with the company.

Unbeknownst to me when I joined the company as a comptroller was that there was a power play going on as to who was going to take over. The competition was between the VP of sales and marketing and the CFO that I reported to. Just a few months after I started, the CFO came up to me as I was preparing the quarterly financial statements for an upcoming board meeting. The numbers were turning out a little better than we had originally thought, so he looked at it and was checking and checking. Finally, he said, "Well, I want you to book a half million dollars in commission expense."

I said, "Okay, for what? Why?"

He said, "I don't care. Call it an accrual bleeding. You know the VP of sales, he will spend it anyhow."

And I said, "Oh, really? Okay." And I thought, "What did I get myself into?"

The last thing I'm going to do is cook the books. I thought this job was a mistake and I decided to leave. But I also had to spread truth, so I prepared two sets of financial statements, the one the CFO wanted with the crude bleeding, and the real statements. I asked *the auditor to come over and look at my work to make sure mine was right. I told him what was happening, and that I was going to deliver two sets of financial statements to the owner of the company. I told him that I was resigning. And he said, "No, no, no. Don't you dare."*

So he went and talked not only to the owner, but to the VP of sales and marketing. The VP of sales and marketing said, "By God, don't let that guy leave." So the auditor said to me, "The board meeting is on Tuesday. I want you to be gone that day." So I said, "Okay, I will be gone, but I'm going to be gone." And he said, "No, no. Nobody is going to accept your resignation at this point." So I said, "Okay."

At the board meeting my boss was let go. The point of this story is you only have integrity once. If you give up your integrity, it is a slippery slope. The chances of getting it back are not very high. And so you only have it once. And that was my trial, whether I was going to keep it, have integrity, or whether I was going to go down a different path.

I have told that story to a fair number of young people and they have said it has really affected their lives. So when coming to those kinds of crossroads and going, you only have integrity once.

Paul is a real champion of being an inspiring guide dog along the journey of life because he really does care for people, has unquestioned integrity, and wants the best for each person. He sees the talent and helps guide the person to where they will excel.

Dennis Doyle, CEO and Chairman of Welsh Companies

Learning how to effectively coach people gave Dennis Doyle an effective leadership style that made Minneapolis-based Welsh Companies a success. He co-founded Welsh in 1977, and served as CEO from 1987 to 2010. Now he is the executive chairman of the board for Welsh Property Trust & Holdco.

Dennis is also the founder and chief executive officer of Hope for the City, a privately funded, non-profit organization established to fight poverty, hunger, and disease by using corporate surplus.

Dennis' high EQ allowed him to focus on growing the talents of his workers instead of giving them all the answers. He has found the secret to nourishing employees: give them the freedom to make up their own minds.

Leadership for me was a very natural thing because I played a lot of sports when I was a kid. I came from a family that really stressed hard work and when you get hurt, you shake it off; even rub some dirt on it. So working on the team I realized that you have to put yourself last, and you have to put your team up front. You must help them in every way that you can. Let the people that are working for you do their jobs and let them do it really well by developing a strong team culture and giving them the freedom to make decisions without fear of making mistakes.

I served as a mentor mainly by walking around the office twice a day talking with pretty much anybody who was available, from secretaries on up. In this way I could get to know my team and get a feel for where the company was, what was going on, who was struggling, and who was doing well. When people wanted feedback, I never told them what to do. I emphasized their freedom to decide how to handle things. I told them, "You know who your client is, how would you handle it?" They usually gave back an answer ten times better than I could come up with anyway!

So my role was not that of an answer man, I was really just engaging our people in their business, and letting them feel confident that they could make mistakes, and nobody is going to fire them. I encouraged them aggressively to do everything they personally could do to take care of their client. Their client was everything. They did not need to do a long list of things to make extra money for the company, they just need to do one thing—make sure that their client was represented as well as he possibly could be. If they did that, then business success would follow naturally.

I noticed that the confidence of each team depended in part on the respect they had for their leaders. For example, we learned a lot about one of our brokerage department leaders on the golf course one day. Our brokers are a very fun group, very entrepreneurial, and they make a lot of money. They're the basis of how our company runs. They are also very competitive, even at a charity golf tournament. All the brokers were standing around as the new manager is coming through to tee off. He hit the ball really well and it landed about 20 feet from the hole.

All of a sudden one of our top brokers shouts out, "Bet you can't make it in two!" The manager got to be about a foot away and then missed again. And you know what? He almost could not recover from it the rest of the round. It was not anything to do with his skill; for he was a talented golfer. It had to do with the lack of confidence from his peers and the fear he had.

Team culture is like that. You really needed to be able to put the ball in the hole when it's your turn. You need to step up at certain times; you need somebody who had your back, particularly the leader of the organization. Leading an organization takes a coaching style of leadership. It is not so much how smart you are or anything else. It is a lot more that you care about people, and can your team put it in the hole at the right time? Can people trust you? People need to know that they make their decisions not based on fear but from the freedom their leader has given them to fail and the confidence that they are vital members of the team.

If you work at instilling confidence in people because they believe in the culture you walk every day, people will exceed your expectations. They will guide you to where you need to be in most cases. And the times when it doesn't turn out the best, you respond with confidence to new solutions rather than in fear.

Parlez-vous Français, Bentley?

Bentley doesn't understand language. Or does he? Some of the best times we have with Bentley are when he tries to communicate with us. He actually guides us so well that it is inspiring. When he was a puppy, I noticed that he listened intently to whatever we were saying. It was like he was taking a crash course on English and figuring out how to communicate what he wanted.

One day I yelled upstairs to Pam that it was time to go somewhere in the car. Bentley immediately got up out of his bed and walked over and stood by the door to the garage. Needless to say, we brought him along although we had not planned to do so.

The next time we spelled it out "C-A-R" and Bentley just stayed put. But then he saw us go to the door and leave. Days later we did the same thing, spelling out the word, but this time Bentley had caught on. He actually got up and went to the door. Yes, we brought him along just because we admired his learning and communication skills. Our Bentley was learning how to spell!

Our final triumph came later when we had to drive somewhere. We fooled Bentley by speaking in French to one another and that took care of it! Bentley did not get up! But the next time we tried it, he again got up and waited by the door for us. Was Bentley becoming bilingual?

We realized that Bentley had not taken an online Berlitz course; he was simply learning our body language as we were preparing to go driving somewhere. He was cuing in to our non-verbal communication. It doesn't seem to matter what language we use, he observes our non-verbal behavior getting ready to leave and goes to the door wanting to go along.

At the same time he is an expert in teaching us *his* non-verbal cues. After we have eaten dinner every night, he will come by one of us and nudge us with his nose and starts getting fidgety. We ask him what he wants and he goes over to the freezer door and waits. This clearly communicates to us that he wants a "dog frosty." If we don't respond, he comes back again and asks with that "please, dad" look in his eyes. He continues with his non-verbal communication until it gets him what he wants. He has learned the art of successful communication without one word!

The Importance of Non-Verbal Communication

That brings us to a key element to being a guide dog and coach to the people you are with every day. We might assume that our main means of communication are through the words we speak and write, but that is not true. We mostly communicate with our hearts, which comes out in our tone of voice, perhaps a warm smile, a touch to the shoulder, a look that makes one laugh, our posture with hands folded or open, and how we look at a person when they are talking to us.

Since non-verbal communication is so important, we need to be aware of how our behavior and body language is sending signals to everyone. If we control our non-verbal communications, we can use this tacit motivational tool to help coach others. What impact might this have on those 70 percent of the people who are disengaged from making a difference at your company or team?

And on the contrary, if you don't pay attention to your non-verbal communication, you might be inadvertently contributing to the alienation of your staff. Here is one example where someone did make a difference by becoming aware of his body language.

I once led a strategy planning session for a company, and anytime there was an opinion expressed by one of the team members that the senior leader did not like, he put his hands across his chest and his face showed his displeasure. When another person piped in and liked the idea, he would get up and walk away for a short time, put his hands on his hips, and tried to hide his anger boiling up.

Fortunately, our fifteen-minute coffee break arrived and I asked the senior leader if we could talk outside briefly. I simply described what I was seeing and asked him how he would feel if his boss were doing the same things. He quickly apologized, as he had no idea that his non-verbal communication was coming across so strongly. I suggested he make an effort to listen, take notes, and share what he was hearing from the group when it came to his time to talk.

Taking notes saved the day because it got him to listen rather than judge. He was able to reflect on what he was hearing. In this way, the best suggestions percolated up and the meeting ended with clarity and clear actions steps that everyone bought into.

The solution is quite simple. Why not try Bentley's more positive form of communication and watch how much more fun it is be at work with engaged people!

Talent Exercise

Being a guide dog to others is one of the great callings to anyone who wants to make a difference. Remember, leadership is not a title, it's an attitude.

How well are you doing at bringing other people along the journey so they will look back ten years from now and say, "_____ (your name) really helped influence my life in a positive way and lead me down the right path. He/she made a lasting and positive difference"?

Who do you need to email or call to thank for being a wonderful "guide dog" to you? Your action will be a pleasant reward for them and it will make their day!

What can you do today to help others be more of who they can become and be truly engaged?

Will you take action to discover what talent is needed in a role and put the right talent in the right job? It is fundamental to everyone's success.

Paw Prints To Remember

☙ According to the most recent Gallup organizations research, 70 percent of the workforce is partially or totally disengaged—and that is shocking! You can be an agent of change by being like Bentley and become an inspiring guide dog!

☙ Learning to guide others is the flip side of being coachable. You can help bring others along and make a difference regardless of your title. It really is an attitude!

☙ Performance immediately increases when you match a person's talent (a person's behavioral style, motivating values, and raw talent) with what the job requires for superior performance!

🐾 Your job as a guide dog and coach is to find out what motivates the person and then do those things that bring out the best in the person.

🐾 Instilling confidence in people is one of the great attributes of a guide dog.

🐾 Communicating with passion your vision and culture are keys to leading, and they involve both verbal and non-verbal areas!

CHAPTER 6

START RUNNING WITH JOY! FIND YOUR INNER POOCH

Come Retrieve With Bentley

Bentley is a natural-born retriever. When we throw a ball for him, Bentley loves to run, pick it up, and bring it right back to us. He retrieves the ball with pure joy and with full conviction because he is simply being himself. He shows the same enthusiasm when Pam or I call for him to "Come!" He never simply walks over to meet us. Bentley runs toward us as fast as he can, because he knows we will greet him with love and encouragement. It is like when you have gone on a trip and return home to see your mom and dad, kids, or spouse. The reunion at the airport is full of many hugs, big smiles, and true joy. Bentley has that same high-energy drive to connect with people. There is nothing quite like the unconditional acceptance we receive from those we love and care for.

This intrinsic joy and self-assurance is what life and work can be for all of us when we follow Bentley's lessons for success. Learning and applying these truths will really help us and our teams. Let's review Bentley's five lessons:

1- Hello, Bentley! Know Who You Are.

2- The Gentle Art of Being Bentley! Be Who You Are.

3- Unleashing Your Talents! Practice Learning New Skills.

4- Don't Let It Bother You; Shake It Off and Pick Up Your Poop!

5- Be A Guide Dog! The Joy of Bringing Others Along

Doing What Bentley Does: Doug Kohrs, Former CEO

One outstanding business leader who exemplifies Bentley's leadership lessons is Doug Kohrs, a former CEO of two highly successful medical device companies, Tornier Medical and American Medical Systems. Doug is a true believer in knowing who you are and then being who you are. I asked Doug what lessons he felt others could benefit from.

"Do what Bentley does!" Doug said. "Learning and leadership are indispensible to success. One of the great lessons I learned at an early age was the discipline of asking myself, 'What did I learn this week?'"

In other words, a good week does not necessarily mean that everything went smoothly, but rather shows how well one reacted to the various challenges.

"Many times, we learned the most when 'crap happened' and then we figured out what are we learning through all of what is happening and how we can best respond. This allowed us to learn more and get to the root cause."

But if his week had been filled with uneventful budget

meetings and he hadn't learned much, he would have intuitively felt that this was not a great week.

One of Doug's key talents is his ability to be rational in the thick of a storm and keep a calm head. When a problem arose or when he was deliberating on a decision that needed to be made, Doug automatically ran the scenarios through his mind of what might happen: What would be the potential disasters? How could I effectively deal with these scenarios so I could avoid the trap? How can I work through the situation with minimal damage? This intellectual skill was a trait that avoided major problems, especially because he was in the medical business and decisions could have a major impact on patients and their loved ones. Doug is thankful his companies avoided devastating issues that might have ended up hurting people.

Leadership Is Not a Title, It's an Attitude!

Early in Doug's career he worked as a budding project engineer in Boston for the medical division of Johnson & Johnson. His team was having great success with their initial product, so J & J saw Doug's potential. They wanted to expand Doug's leadership and develop his skills, so they told him to go hire an engineer. At the time, Doug was only twenty-six and this was to be his first hire. He looked for the right talent and interviewed Jude, a young engineer from MIT, one of the best engineering schools in the world. Jude was just twenty-two, but Doug thought that he had great potential, so he hired him. Jude and Doug thus began a highly successful relationship, and came up with more ideas that worked.

Since this was all new to Doug, he didn't realize you could be a leader without anyone working for you. He just wanted to make a difference. Doug viewed Jude as a colleague, not as a subordinate. The two of them simply focused on the goal at hand and enjoyed working together to get the job done. In fact, the other people in the company did not necessarily know who the boss was because Doug and Jude were so focused on having fun with their many successful projects.

Let's now fast-forward to today, thirty years later. Doug serves on six different boards and is consulting with one of the giant med-tech companies working on a big project to change health care and delivery. When Doug has a problem to think over, guess who he calls up? You guessed it. He and Jude are back working as a team.

"I am treating Jude the same as I did thirty years ago at J & J—as colleagues," said Doug.

Just like Bentley, Doug and Jude each know their own talents and come together "being who they are" with no thought as to who is the boss, but how can they change the world together!

What is amazing is that Doug repeated the same formula for hiring at another med-tech company, but this time the engineer had no formal education, just street talent as a mechanical engineer. Doug saw his work, witnessed his "can do" attitude and the two of them worked together for years to improve patients' lives. Doug pointed out that one successful engineer came from a top university and the other came with no formal education, just natural ability. The common denominator was talent and the passion to make a difference. It's back to the fundamental belief that "leadership is not a title, it's an attitude."

Chris Wright, President of the Timberwolves and Lynx

When you meet Chris Wright and hear his British accent, you can't help but smile. He is such a sincere and engaging person with a drive for success. Chris comes from the small town of Filey in England and has always had a love for sports. He found his way to Minnesota and ended up working for the Minnesota Timberwolves' original owners, Harvey Ratner and his partner Marv Wolfenson.

When businessman Glen Taylor bought the team in 1996, Chris was the only executive retained. He worked for the new ownership group for one year under his old contract. When his one-year contract expired, he called Glen Taylor and asked, "What do you want me to do?"

Glen immediately replied that he would come to the Timberwolves office and meet with him.

When they met, Chris said he would like to work under another contract since he has always worked under one in the past. Glen told him he did not want to put Chris on a contract, but went on to say that after seeing how Chris treated his staff and clients and how he lead people and built great relationships, he wanted to offer the following: "I want you to lead our business operation and run things for us. I won't let you down as long as you don't let me down. Don't worry about a contract, I'll never let your family down."

Glen put out his hand and emphatically told Chris he wanted to have him continue on and they shook hands. Glen launched Chris into an exciting role because Glen saw the talent, trust, and unique qualities that Chris brought to the Timberwolves organization. It was a great fit for both of them.

It is now seventeen years later and Chris Wright is still working for Glen Taylor as the president of both the Timberwolves and the Lynx. This was all on a handshake from someone who saw the great match between Chris' talent and the job. Chris is a great example of someone who knew he had a passion for the responsibilities he was being offered, and learned to know and grow his talents.

Recently, Glen was considering selling the teams. But once Flip Saunders became available as the new GM to run the Timberwolves, Glen knew it was the wrong time to sell, and just as important, he felt with the team's performance heading in the right direction, he could start having fun again!

Chris had always told Glen that if he sold the team and left, he would leave also. So when Glen walked in one day after making up his mind not to sell, he said to Chris,"If we don't sell the team for another for three or four years, will you stay?"

The answer was easy: "Yes!" Such decisions are so much easier when you are following your passion, know your talents, use them on a daily basis, and work with people you trust and respect.

So where are your passions? Do you know your talents today? This is the essence of finding your "sweet spot" and taking your talents to a new level. To launch effectively for yourself and your team members, you start with knowing and being who you are. It is at this point that you can unleash your God-given talents, face down those areas of disappointment, shake off your problems, and become a guide dog for others.

Chris Wright didn't simply develop his own talents. As a talented leader, he knew that success depends on nourishing the talents of all his employees. He says he is most proud of how he has been able to develop and provide a culture where people can grow and excel.

"My key stakeholders are my 167 members on my staff. So I try to put them at the center of everything I do on a day-to-day basis because the better I can make them, so goes our franchise."

He doesn't hire people just for skill sets; one must also fit into the Timberwolves/Lynx culture. He wants each employee to be a brand ambassador for the team. Chris' approach has always been to find out what the customers' needs are and help them accomplish their goals. A cookie cutter approach doesn't work. They learn what their consumer really needs and wants, and then align this with how they can help.

One of Chris' greatest achievements is how his people have developed and grown in the Timberwolves culture. Some have grown so much they were recruited away by other companies and have launched new careers. Some examples include the president of the Cleveland Cavaliers, the president of the Sacramento Kings, and most recently the Chief Revenue Officer for the new San Francisco 49ers.

How can this culture be so effective? Chris, in part, credits the "One program" that is an onboarding process committed to "One" team, "One" community, "One" voice that the Wolves have developed for their new employees.

They take onboarding seriously. Every new employee has lunch with Chris and the senior management team. Each person is assigned a mentor for one year to help him or her get launched and understand the Timberwolves and Lynx brand and culture.

As part of the "One" program, they also do a 30-60-90 follow up with human resources and a meeting with Chris after six months and one year. This is to assure that the organization is doing what it said it would do and to understand the team member's own aspirations. Chris asks them four questions:

What was it like when we onboarded you?

What were the first two weeks like?

What were the next five months like?

What do you aspire or want to do in the next six months?

The systematic culture that enables talent to flourish is successful. All of this allows employees to become Brand Ambassadors for the Timberwolves and the Lynx. Chris embodies Bentley's core leadership lessons!

It is Time Now To Look At Your Paw Prints!

I took Bentley out today for a walk through one of the most beautiful, wooded trails in Eden Prairie, Minnesota. It is a place called Birch Island. You park your car and walk onto the paths that wind gently through the woods. It is like a slice of heaven—calm, beautiful, and it makes you feel so free. Bentley runs back and forth on the path and veers off certain side paths that we know so well together.

I want you to imagine for a moment that you are on this beautiful path with a canopy of large trees that sets the stage as you walk through the woods, hearing occasional birds singing out their songs. **You have graciously invited me and Bentley to join you for a short walk in this Birch Island sanctuary.**

You begin by asking me the following question: "Robb, I have had real success thus far in my career but I know there is much more to do and become. Where might I gain insight?"

Robb: "Our calling and purpose is a natural extension of our talents and pure passion. Try going back to Chapter 1 and invest time discovering who you truly are. There is gold in your many God-given gifts, so let's figure out what they are! The exercises are a start but you may want to go further and do a full battery of leader assessments including Emotional Intelligence, so you can discover more inborn talents to use at work and in life."

As we walk further down the path, you ask me another question: "When you talked about how Bentley gets out of the water and shakes himself until the water is gone, it seems easy in concept, but I have some heartache with a few people from the past. Is this important to deal with or is this just a normal part of life?"

Robb: "First, it is 100 percent normal to know a few people that you don't want to be around and have some angst when you see them or hear their names. You simply need to understand that you don't have to be friends with these people by extending forgiveness. Forgiveness is first for you so that you are free from encumbrances and so you can fully enjoy the walk through life without carrying bitterness or worry. You may want to share with these people that you forgive them and leave it at that. However, the better way is to begin a conversation with them and be understanding of their situations. This costs you nothing financially, but allows you to be free of unwanted negative emotions that can drag you down. Take a look again at Chapter 4."

As we near the end of the path, you ask me your final question: "I have tried to help people who've worked for me in the past in various ways, but I can't say I am an inspiring 'guide dog.' Any advice?"

Robb: "It is great to hear your honesty, and I can tell by your question that you want to make a difference and become an inspiring 'guide dog' for others. If you know your talents and focus on what is in Chapter 2, which is all about being who you are, your genuine relationship with others lays the foundation to gain wisdom in how to best guide those people. Our role as leaders is to find out what motivates people and then help them bring out their best talents so they can reach their goals. In learning how to be an inspiring guide dog, you in turn will be inspired. It is the law of sowing good seed and reaping the harvest in due time. When you see someone struggling, asking great questions will help them discover the answers."

The Wrap Up

Think back and remind yourself of the simple concepts you can learn from my dog Bentley. He truly lights up my life every day in so many ways. When I come home, there he is with his tail wagging, doing his magically happy greeting. We have much to learn from animals like Bentley and can apply this natural wisdom to everyday life. I know that information without insight is stagnation. When you are honest with yourself, you can embrace change with Bentley's leadership lessons and discover the greatness that is in YOU! You will do it if you take action!

I WILL BEGIN MAKING A NEW PAWPRINT BY TAKING THESE ACTIONS:

1.

2.

3.

Paw Prints to Remember

The following questions will help you tackle this challenge: What is one step you can take to further your own paw print for life?

🐾 Will you now take action to rediscover your talents, motivating values, and strengths of your style? The brief exercises are here to give you a start and be like kindling to a fire that wants to bust forth.

🐾 What talents from your mini-360 do you want to start using a lot more and get better at?

🐾 What coaching do you need at this point? What skill development is needed? Just pick one and begin!

🐾 Is there any area you need to shake off, like Bentley does when he comes out of the water? Taking action toward resolving any past issues will bring peace to you, and the freedom to become what you *can* become.

🐾 Who do you know on your journey who needs more guidance? Do you have room in your heart for someone else? If so, email them about what you are learning and see what may come about!

GO, BENTLEY!
GO, YOU!
AND BEST WISHES ON YOUR NEW PATH!